The
Sweet Spot

Everything Women Need to Know
to Enjoy Life More

Copyright © 2020 by Kacie Vaudrey
All rights reserved. No part of this book may be reproduced in any form or by any means—electronic, mechanical, photocopying, or scanning—without written permission from the author except by reviewers who may quote.

Kacie Vaudrey LLC
www.KacieVaudrey.com

Publisher's Cataloging-In-Publication Data

Names: Vaudrey, Kacie, author.
Title: The sweet spot : everything women need to know to enjoy life more / Kacie Vaudrey.
Description: [Park City, Utah] : Kacie Vaudrey LLC, [2019]
Identifiers: ISBN 9781734082708 (paperback) | ISBN 9781734082715 (ebook)
Subjects: LCSH: Happiness. | Women—Conduct of life. | Quality of life. | Self-care, Health.
Classification: LCC BF575.H27 V38 2019 (print) | LCC BF575.H27 (ebook) | DDC 158.1082—dc23

Printed in the United States of America

This publication is designed to provide accurate and authoritative information with regard to the subject matter covered. It is sold with the understanding that neither the author nor the publisher is engaged in rendering legal, accounting, or other professional advice. If legal advice or other expert assistance is required, the services of a competent professional person should be sought.

To Mike and our children for supporting me on the journey to realizing how important it is to live in the space of the sweet spot

PRAISE

"Kacie Vaudrey is one of the most caring, compassionate, and intelligent women I know. She's a visionary who, once inspired, commits and takes action. She is surely someone you want to surround yourself with if your path is to grow."
—Hayley Hobson, Health & Life Coach

"Kacie Vaudrey is a very fun and passionate leader. She has a genuine heart to love and care for people. I like her no-nonsense, get-on-with-it attitude. Most importantly, anyone would do well if they can adopt her can-do attitude."
—Jade Balden, Educator, Energy Healer, Author of *Pink Jade: A True Story of a Vietnamese Refugee Girl* and *Love, Light, & Healing: A Reference Guide to Energy Balancing with Faith*

"In a world where feeling unworthy is probably the number one problem for women, Kacie Vaudrey makes them feel worthy. Whenever I need a boost or encouragement, Kacie is always there. Believing in me. Pushing me. Helping me formulate new ideas. Telling me I can be greater than I am. Truthfully. The way she believes in me, lifts me up, encourages me, and supports my team is invaluable. I'm so lucky to have Kacie in my life and business."
—Megan Winfrey, CEO of Essentially Oils and Share the Love

"In the time I worked with Kacie Vaudrey, I witnessed her immense passion for others . . . it's palatable! She embodies a level of authenticity and vulnerability that's truly a breath of fresh air."

—Brittany Bayley, Founder and CEO of Email Copy School

CONTENTS

Chapter 1. The Sweet Spot Effect 1

Chapter 2: Clear the Baggage 15

Chapter 3: Yes, You Do Deserve It 33

Chapter 4: Yes, You Can Feel Fear and Act Anyway 59

Chapter 5: Forever Enough 69

Chapter 6: The Surprising Truth about Expectations ... 81

Chapter 7: Who's on Your Team? 89

Chapter 8: Sweeten the Spot 99

About the Author 112

CHAPTER 1
THE SWEET SPOT EFFECT

Your kids are in college, or they will be soon. You've bought the car. You've traveled to Paris. You live in your dream home. Your vision board is complete. Now what? Are the good days over? Is there no more dreaming? No more aspiring for more?

    Nah. Far from it, sister. It's time to sweeten the deal. Time to bring in more of the little things that give you the most joy, make the biggest impact, and let you live life to the fullest. I like to think of this as your second chance. Why else would we live to be ninety if it wasn't for the sheer fact we *deserve* to get things right? We're smarter, more experienced, and more prepared now for anything and everything that comes our way. We're ready for the good life. And we deserve it.

Remember when we used to daydream about stuff and trips and the finer things in life? We dreamt of having a career, owning a home, buying a car, losing weight, and traveling around the world. That feels like ages ago. Over time, we've gotten a lot of what we want. We've achieved. We've mastered. We've raised (or are raising) kids. Now our dreams are different. They aren't so specific. We don't plan out our dreams or glue them to a board. Nowadays we're not wondering, *How do I find the partner of my dreams and a white picket fence?* You're asking yourself, *Why doesn't Victoria's Secret carry nighties that cover my butt so I can celebrate my anniversary without feeling like a whale?!*

Life has happened. Now what?

I used to love vision boards . . . when I was thirty. And between you and me, I still have one. Yet in my forties, a vision board isn't getting me any closer to the things I want or need. Maybe because the things that fire me up don't exist in a magazine ad. They come from my heart. I can fulfill them in a split second with the right people. We already have so many of the things we've aspired to. Now we care more about the little things.

But that's not what we're *supposed* to care about. Read any self-help books recently? Every author, speaker, and trainer says, "Dream bigger!" I get it. I learned from the best of these individuals. Don't get me wrong—I'm still a dreamer. I wouldn't have written this book if I wasn't. But this book isn't about dreaming big. It's about using everything we've learned to get what we want in life.

Let's talk dreaming for a second. When I was a girl, I wanted to travel in a BMW convertible with my soul mate. Mind you, I grew up in Wyoming, where I rarely saw a person drive, let alone own a convertible. It was a fantasy of the unknown that filled my heart. The same as finding my soul mate. Today my fantasies are my reality.

The first time my soul mate and I rode in our convertible with the top down, I felt like I'd "made it." That dream feels like it was ages ago. It was a goal, a marker representing success. I'm not living in that same space now. I had dreams that evolved. They kept evolving and evolving. Now as I look to my future, I want to dream different dreams. Time is sweet. It gives us that second chance in life to learn from both our successes and our screwups. We can turn our experiences into our happiness. We can take what we want and make it a reality. Isn't that what living is all about?

Maybe life's simple pleasures aren't good enough for the naysayers. You know they're out there. Maybe they're close to you. In your home. *In your head.* What if you don't see yourself traveling the world again (or for the first time)? What if you only want to be happy? What if your "big dream" is as simple as getting up early and enjoying a fresh cup of coffee? Watching the sunset and listening to Coldplay on your deck a couple of times a week? Going on a kid-free date with your partner once a month?

"Dream bigger!" we're reminded. Cue the guilt. So we create the vision board. We clip airbrushed photos from *Cosmo* of slim waists and big houses. We write affirmations from the motivational book everyone keeps talking about. Then our girlfriends come over. They see our finished product. And they laugh.

"You want *all that*?" says a friend. "Wow . . . I'm just . . . I'm surprised. Aren't you happy with everything you already have? I don't know. I guess if I went after things like that, I'd feel a little selfish." Selfish. The magic word that sends us reeling back to mediocrity and closes the dream book with a bang.

Guilt round two. Behind the cabinet goes the vision board. Your kids never see it. You definitely don't show it to your spouse. *When the kiddos graduate*, you think, *then I can dream again . . .*

As women, we're expected to play a game we're not allowed to win. We're supposed to be the perfect woman. *Have* it all, but not *want* it all. That would just be greedy. It's like everyone's waiting to pounce, judge, and compare. Conflicted much? I can't be the only one who sees a problem here.

The people around you—loved ones, coworkers, other moms at yoga—they don't always come out and say it. But you feel their expectations. You're supposed to be this strong, beautiful, independent woman with a fulfilling career of your own *and* somehow also be an amazing mother, awesome spouse, and perfect cook. And don't forget the spotless house. If we don't aspire to embody this ideal female image, something must be wrong with us. We're supposed to do *whatever* the hustle requires, sacrificing "me time" for something bigger than ourselves. If we don't "make it," our family, our friends, and the teenage cashier at the grocery store see us as a failure. Even though they're all living in the same hamster wheel we are. To top it off, if our partner is cranky, if our kid gets called to the principal's office (and even the perfect ones do), or if we forget to clean the mud off the kitchen floor, we're *a bad mom . . . a bad wife . . . a bad person.* You gave everything you had to everyone who expected it, and you've got nothing to show for it but a half-empty bottle of cheap wine. Yes, I'm speaking from experience.

Here's a little secret about those external expectations—you can live up to them and still feel miserable. Come on—think of that one couple you know. The one who has it all. You know who I'm talking about.

The Sweet Spot

You feel a little guilty when they're around. Because you're envious. They have a multimillion-dollar home. They're always in shape. They take lavish vacations four times a year. They're always writing big checks to good causes. They dress to the latest trend. And did I mention their perfect white teeth?

But do you remember the last time you saw them? You didn't see those teeth, did you? No genuine smiles. I bet they didn't kiss or hold hands. They probably didn't even sit together. They have *everything*, but they're not happy. Is that what you want?

If you're anything like me, you just want to let your hair down once in a while. You want to splurge on a gluten-filled muffin at the coffee shop guilt-free or order another pair of your favorite jeans without asking permission. If you have younger children, you just want more sleep. Teens in the house? It's all you can do to get thirty minutes for a bath once a week without them banging on the door. These aren't big dreams. They're little things that just make you happy.

You know the thing about these little moments? They change you. Even if only for a few minutes afterward. You're happier. You're lighter. You're in "the flow." Beneath those bubbles in the bath, you feel like *you* again. The person you always wished you could be. You feel like you're in the right place at the right time. You're not thinking about what you're supposed to do or who you're supposed to be. You're not overhauling your life, moving into a mansion, or finding a new partner. Yet you're happy. Just. Happy. You know you can go out there and show up as your best self. You've found your sweet spot, and you wish you could stay there forever. Then life happens. Sigh. You get out of the bath. The kids are fighting. The dishes aren't done. Somebody needs to walk the dog. *Goodbye, sweet spot. Hello, reality.*

What if it didn't have to be that way? What if you could return to that place of genuine happiness—your sweet spot—and stay there? *Forever.* Imagine your life full of these refreshing moments. These little things that just make you happy. Not once a week or every few months, but throughout the day *every single day*.

Yeah, right. If I take an hour every night for a bath, that's an hour of productivity I lose, you may be thinking. *One hour in my sweet spot is one hour lost doing something for my kids, my husband, my church, my friends, my job . . .*

Stop.

You're not trading off, you're trading up. The time you give yourself changes how you show up in bed with your spouse, with your kids the next morning, and at work the next day. When you disrupt your routine—and expectations—to do those little things that just make you happy, the impact is far and above what you gave up.

Those little rushes compound. Soon, you have a surplus of joy. You can't *help* but become a more refreshed version of yourself—the *you* you've always wanted to be. Your sanity returns. You get the self-confidence those self-help books promise. You're ready for whatever life throws at you.

Here's the thing. The sweet spot looks different for everyone. It's not a comparison. If yours isn't a convertible or coffee, maybe it's journaling, reading, going to the movies, or meditating. Maybe it's getting a manicure or even gardening. I get into my sweet spot when I put the coffee on, work out, brush the horses, feed the chickens, listen to an audiobook, go hiking, plant flowers, take a bubble bath, and immerse myself in my business. It's not making a ton of money every minute that makes me happy. It's simply doing the right activity to move in the right direction with no resistance. And it doesn't have to be perfect. I give myself a lot of grace because I know *nothing* we do is ever perfect. All that matters is action. That's what brings balance and peace. And that balance and peace changes everything (and everyone) you touch.

When I get my coffee in the morning, I set an intention—*I will be kind to my family.* I took care of myself; now I take care of them. I don't snap at my kids for petty things like crusty dishes or dirty socks. I treat my husband how he wants to be treated, and he does the same for me. We take care of each other. We put each other first. As parents, we make decisions that make sense, and our kids respect them. We're not pitting ourselves against each other's defiance. We're working in a partnership. All because I took the time to get my freaking coffee. *That*, sister, is the Sweet Spot Effect.

The Sweet Spot Effect: a perpetual state of satisfaction caused by consistently doing little things that just make you happy

The Sweet Spot Effect is for everyone, not just for the privileged few. Anyone can get out of their comfort zone to enjoy the little things that just make them happy. Take my mom. Every Tuesday, she golfs. It's her thing. She's not disrupting the family finances. She's not going out saving the world. She's coming home refreshed and happier. That's what the sweet spot is all about.

Let's be real. If indulging in the sweet spot were as easy as, "I'm just going to play golf all the time!" we'd do it . . But it's not. And we'd feel better . . . And we don't. Why not? Why don't we make time for those little things that just make us happy? Those dirty little expectations, that's why. As women, we've designed our entire adult lives around obligations. We're not *supposed* to be taking that bubble bath because we're *supposed* to be reading eighteen thousand books to our kids before they go to bed. And then we fall asleep only to wake up the next morning in the same vicious cycle we call life.

But what if taking care of everyone (and everything) in your world meant taking care of *you* first? What if there was a new way to live that took us to that sweet spot and kept us there—even when we're surrounded by clutter, chaos, and drama? And what if I wrote this book to tell you all about it?

INTENTIONAL LIVING: THE ANTIDOTE TO OBLIGATION

I'm just going to say it. You deserve those little things that just make you happy. That's the *what*. The *how* is Intentional Living. Intentional Living means getting clear on what fulfills you and then restructuring your day to incorporate it. It's a lifestyle shift that drives you, feeds your soul, and keeps you moving. When you live intentionally, everything happens on purpose. The conversations you have. The people you hang out with. The way you spend money. The career choice you make. The food you put in your body. The way you exercise. It's all intentional, supportive, and fulfilling.

Best of all, Intentional Living is practical. You don't have to take crazy leaps where you forget all responsibility, end every toxic relationship, and pack up your belongings. However, that doesn't mean Intentional Living is easy. That's why I'm here, friend. The fact that you picked up this book tells me you're still looking for hope in the world. You still want something better for yourself and for everyone around you.

This book will teach you how to get back to your sweet spot, stay there, and bring your loved ones with you. My goal is to make the sweet spot—and whatever it takes to get you there—your norm. Part of your life. Who you are. My friends always tell me, "Kacie, you take such good care of yourself." Honestly? It's all I know in this second life of mine. I'm not perfect. Far from it. Yet I know the moment I leave my sweet spot, I turn into a whack job. I get a headache. I get stuck in a funk. I yell at my kids. *Whoa, where'd* that *monster come from? Reel it back in, Kacie.* I don't just love living in my sweet spot. I can't afford to leave.

This book tells many stories about finding, losing, and rediscovering both the little and big things that bring me bliss. Even the raw stories I've never told in public. But like my sweet spot, this book isn't just about me. I'm a ray of hope. I'm here to make you laugh, cry, and force yourself to get off your behind, take massive action, and reclaim your sweet spot, whatever that may be. If you see what a good day looks like, I'll help you make it a reality. And if you're smart, you'll find people to join in the fun.

I have but one rule. No people-pleasing allowed. Seriously. No busting your butt for something you couldn't care less about. No envying other people. Let go of the life the world would have you live. It's time you remember the little things that just make you happy, and it's time to go get them. Because guess what? There's more to this life than everything you've known so far. As you fulfill your little desires, you'll work your way up to bigger dreams you're too scared to admit you have right now. Everyone tells you to start big, go big, and stay big. I'm telling you to start small, have fun, and stay consistent. Soon you'll write your own success story, whether that's getting all the sleep you need or running a multimillion-dollar business from home if that's your thing.

Even though everyone's sweet spot looks different, every step to reach and remain in your sweet spot is the same as everyone else's. We're on this journey together. We all want habits that work for us, not against us, a routine that refreshes us, not wears us down, and relationships that enrich us, not deplete us. Follow every step of Intentional Living and you'll automatically arrive in your sweet spot. You literally can't help but get there.

The steps we'll take to make the sweet spot your natural habitat include:

- Disrupting expectations without burning bridges
- Developing the confidence to say what you mean and go after what you want
- Celebrating your victories, even the tiny ones like getting up without hitting snooze once
- Cutting the BS guilt that masquerades as gratitude
- Upgrading your circle of influence to support the woman you want to become
- Setting realistic expectations so you can do what everyone else just talks about
- Turning adversity into opportunity and failures into fuel for what's next
- Integrating self-care into every moment without feeling self-centered
- Raising your personal standards (and your self-respect)

The first step on our journey to the sweet spot is to step around what's blocked us from getting there. I'm talking fears, expectations, and excuses that keep you out of the bubble bath every freaking time you think about it. Clear that baggage out of the way and you're well on your way to your sweet spot. Ready to take the first step with me?

CHAPTER 2
CLEAR THE BAGGAGE

"But."

That word holds us back, blocks out happiness, and keeps us trapped in a cycle of put-yourself-last. You know what I'm talking about. "But" is the little witch on your shoulder. She whispers, "But you don't deserve success," when you've worked hard. "But you don't have enough time," when you get a free half hour to yourself. And, "But you don't have the skills," when you start a business or pursue your dream career.

"But."

She's mean. She's ruthless. She's relentless. I used to think she was my voice of reason. My safety net that kept me from doing all the stupid things my gut urged me to do. I know better now. That little witch on our shoulder says whatever she must to keep you and me out of the sweet spot.

And for most of my adult life, it worked. Not because I went around excusing myself from success or objecting to good reasons to take care of me. I *liked* the little witch. Whenever I'd get an idea to disrupt expectations, get out of my comfort zone, or do something for me, "but" came rushing to my aid. "But" kept me safe from rejection, from disappointment, and from failure. It also kept me from living. I could want something like ditching a toxic partner to find my soul mate. The second I listened to the little witch's chatter, it was over. *Oh, you're right. I want love, but I don't deserve it. Guess I'll stay in this miserable relationship until I die.*

Relate much? I know you do. Society expects women to accept excuses that get in the way of what we want. Carrying baggage is our rite of passage into adulthood. We've all met the woman who gets sick because she's so busy keeping her kids healthy. Who goes broke putting food on the table for an ungrateful, deadbeat spouse. Who burns out taking care of aging loved ones. Maybe that woman is you. Whatever your story is, I'm guessing it hasn't reached a hopeful plot twist yet, much less a happy ending. The beauty is, it's not over. It's not too late to ditch that baggage. It's *never* too late.

To get that witch off your shoulders, we first have to know how she got there. Why is it *so dang hard* to take thirty minutes for a bath or to save an extra hundred dollars in a fun-money fund? Why does objecting to our own happiness come *so easy*? It's not you, girlfriend. It's your brain. Any traumas or stresses you've experienced in your life stir up emotions, which, in time, settle into your belief system.[1]

As a former university professor, I'm all about an evidence-based approach to every area of life. That includes how to fix your mindset so you can do little things that make you happy baggage-free. Now, this isn't a psychology textbook. But feelings create beliefs. Like those that give your little witch permission to camp out on your shoulder. That's why I can't resist introducing you to one of my favorite expert witch removers. Here's what psychology professor William Gibson, PhD, has to say about ditching your baggage:

> We respond to experiences emotionally and carry our perceived view of the consequences with us into new experiences. We seek to learn from our past

---

[1] Nico H. Frijda, Anthon S. R. Manstead, and Sacha Bem, eds., *Emotions and Beliefs: How Feelings Influence Thoughts* (Cambridge: Cambridge University Press), 2000.

experiences, which . . . includes carrying forward threatening and unhealthy "baggage." It is a component of human development to carry our personal perception of our past experience with us ... We often are influenced by past emotional experiences in how we interpret and perceive current personal interactions and primary relationships. Our relationships with others often include emotional responses and our responses are likely to be prejudiced, both positively and negatively, by past experiences.[2]

Dr. Gibson is describing pattern recognition, a process in which our brains match what we *experience* to what we *remember*.[3] Every woman alive has pattern-matched herself into misery. If some heartless bully manager at your first job told you, "You don't have what it takes to make it here," guess what, sister? The bite of those words loosened over the years, but their impression on you did not. When you started a side business from home, what feeling couldn't you shake? *I want this. I need this. But I don't have what it takes to make*

---

[2] Brianna Steinhilber, "Is Your Emotional Baggage Holding You Back?" NBC News, July 24, 2018, www.nbcnews.com/better/health/your-emotional-baggage-holding-you-back-ncna877596.

[3] Marsha S. Corrigan, *Pattern Recognition in Biology* (New York: Nova Science), 2007.

it. Why am I even doing this? I will never succeed. Boom. Pattern matched. Your little "but" witch crapped all over your business dreams.

Maybe you feel guilty because you don't think you have enough time to be supermom, superwife, and superwoman in your career. You feel you're under a spotlight, performing for everyone in your life. You must compete. Push. Make everyone happy. Except you.

I get it. It's hard to clear that baggage, no matter how you ended up with it. But you *can*. That's the good news. Like I said earlier, the sweet spot is for everyone. Are you going to let that little witch continue to sit on your shoulder, or are you going to evict her and all the baggage she makes you carry? All those experiences distort the reasons you should do those little things that just make you happy. Uncleared baggage builds a wall between you and your sweet spot. Even worse? Stack it in the exact wrong place and it can kill you.

TIME IS TICKING: CLEAR THE BAGGAGE OR I'M DEAD

The cough. How long have I had this cough?

Something wasn't right. I was in no condition to find out, and the fear of knowing scared me to death. Literally. I'll keep this simple. At the time, my husband was moving out. Things weren't good. We rarely spoke. When we did, we yelled. Our marriage was full of hate and dysfunction that trickled down to our two young kids. I could see and feel the toll it was taking on them. On me. We tried to "work on our marriage," but honestly there wasn't much to work on. Somehow after fifteen years of being together, we couldn't figure each other out. So I threw in the towel. He wasn't the man I needed or wanted anymore. We had married when I was twenty-three. I grew up, but our relationship didn't.

Starting over at thirty-eight isn't easy. It isn't at any age. Tail between my legs, I asked my parents for money to make ends meet. Their cash infusion I was humbled enough to ask for wasn't enough to keep a formerly two-income household running. So I threw myself into teaching more classes on campus. I also committed to building a multilevel marketing business. *Gulp.*

Failure is crippling. It's not something I can describe with ease. I will say one thing. The personal damage it causes isn't something the heart deals with well. For months I angry-cried myself to sleep every night. *Why me? No one else I know is divorced. Who will love me? I'm useless. I'm not worthy of anything good anymore.* Every horrible thing I could tell myself, I did. The witch was in control. I was paralyzed. Night after night, I pleaded with my higher power to give me strength. Nothing. *God, it's your chance. Wake up and help a girl out. Seriously.*

My emotional health was in the dumps. Physical health was close behind. On March 6, 2013, I curled up on my shower floor and lost it. I knew that day my life would change. The lump in my breast told me so. *Thank you, lump. So glad you could show up for the PAR-TAY.*

It's ironic how life works. I happened to have a mammogram scheduled that day. No kidding. I guess my higher power was awake and working. I'd started getting routine checkups at age thirty-five. That's what you do when you lose a grandmother and an aunt at thirty-eight to breast cancer. I cancelled my appointment the year prior because I felt fine. And I sure didn't feel like getting my boobs squished in a machine. Who wants to be in that awkward situation unless you have to? My doctor said checkups were optional. *Optional.* I took that to heart.

March 6 kicked off my first week off in a while, and I was looking forward to sleeping in with the kids and playing hooky all day. Then I saw the appointment on my calendar. *Ugh.* I knew in my heart I needed to go, but I called to cancel my appointment anyway. My heart was heavy. I couldn't bear the news I knew I'd receive. The only problem was, I let slip on the phone that I found a lump. Within minutes, my primary doctor's nurse phoned me back.

"We need to see you today."

Apparently my admission about finding the lump automatically changed the prescription for my mammogram. The system upgraded me to "high risk."

That meant I had to see my primary-care physician before my mammogram.

Our body reacts to what's coming before we do. On the drive to my appointment, I felt numb. Emotionless. A wall formed around my heart so thick the news couldn't shatter it. I was ready to fight, and I didn't even know what I was fighting for. My body knew. My gut knew. And my heart knew.

I walked into the waiting room and signed in at reception. The nurse behind the glass looked up and smiled.

"Hello, how are you doing today?"

"Fine, thanks." A lie. I cleared my throat. "Hey, so . . . a nurse called. I'm here to see a doctor and get my mammogram. There's been a bit of a change because I found . . . *a lump.*"

You know That Look someone gives you when you offend the whole room with what you thought was an innocent joke? The nurse turned to her desk mate, an old guy with a bird's nest for hair. He had on a lab coat. A doctor, I assumed. The nurse whispered something. Doctor Lab Coat swiveled toward reception. Then he shot me That Look. They'd been waiting for me.

"Ma'am, follow me please," the nurse said.

At every previous mammogram appointment, I passed the time catching up on gossip magazines.

Clear the Baggage

"OK." I coughed and grabbed a tissue. We walked into a beautiful, serene dressing space, and she handed me a gown.

"I'll be back to escort you to your exam room in just a minute."

I sat down and waited. Anxiety kicked in. It took everything I had just to breathe. I could hear the clock tick-tocking. I watched other patients enter the dressing room for their appointments. The scene felt so strange—like I was just this body sitting in a chair watching the world happen to me.

The nurse walked into the dressing room to escort me back. The look on her face said what neither of us wanted to think about.

"You're fine," she told me. Again. Then again. Over and over and over again she repeated those two words until for a split second I forgot my turmoil and agreed. *I'm fine.*

"Because you found a lump, there will be additional people in the room," the nurse said. "That includes the radiologist to ensure all images are properly captured."

She was right. The room was packed. I kept my eyes closed for most of the exam. It took ten minutes. The nurse escorted me back to the dressing room afterward.

"Get dressed and wait here. I'll be back to take you into the radiologist's office."

So we went. I felt nothing. The radiologist looked like he wanted to give me a hug. He didn't. Images of my breast blown up appeared on the screen behind him.

"Do you have anyone you want to call?"

I shook my head.

"OK. So we can't confirm this a hundred percent. But we are about ninety-nine percent certain you have breast cancer. We need to schedule a biopsy first thing in the morning. Can you come back?"

When people in movies get this news, they always play a somber piano soundtrack. Instead, I heard Michael Franti crooning from the hallway ceiling speaker about sunshine and love.

I swallowed hard. I already knew something like this was coming. Cancer was in my blood.

I left the hospital and got in my car. I wasn't sure what to do. Cry? Scream? Laugh? Punch something? Why isn't there a crash course on dealing with your imminent death?

I called my parents. My brother. My friends. Word spread fast. I took one call after the next for twelve hours. I felt scared, tired, and mad. And uncertain of what was happening. The strange thing about a cancer diagnosis is that it's easier on the patient than those who sit on the sidelines. The people I looked to for support needed me to step up and surround them in strength and confidence.

I knew I'd fight with my entire being. They weren't so sure. I was OK carrying them through this process. They didn't understand what I felt or how I'd react to their attempts at encouragement anyway. The word "cancer" paralyzed them.

The next couple of days were a blur. Biopsy. Tears. Counseling sessions. Tears. Oncologist. Reality.

"Your cancer is aggressive," my oncologist said at my biopsy appointment.

"How aggressive?" I asked.

"Well, what concerns me is the—the cough. You've had it for six months now?" He looked down at his clipboard. "Yes, so time is critical."

I thought of my Aunt Pam, the one who died at thirty-eight. I remembered the last time I saw her. She didn't catch it soon enough. When she got her diagnosis, the cancer had already metastasized. From breasts to lungs, bones, and brain. Then I thought of my grandmother, whose breast cancer also spread to her lungs. Their deaths left my family devastated. Was that my kids' destiny?

The oncologist's voice softened. "Kacie, at your stage," he said, "the sooner we start treatment, the better your prognosis. Before we go any further and discuss your options, I have to ask, would you like to call somebody? Your husband or a family member?"

"No," I said. "Not right now." I needed to know what I was up against. Then I'd figure it out.

"Oh. I thought . . . I would've guessed . . . I just—" The guy looked panicked. He shuffled some papers, then held up my breast scans. He spoke in a rush. "With the severity and the aggressiveness and the markers and the size of the tumor and your biopsy showing you are HER2 positive—"

"HER2? What's that?"

"HER2 is a gene that basically feeds cancer cells. So even if twelve months of chemo and radiation eliminate cancer from one breast, there is still a possibility that you will come out of remission."

"So . . . the only way to get the cancer out of my body for sure is a double mastectomy?"

"Oh no. I strongly advise against that. Many women feel an attachment to—"

"I feel an attachment to staying alive." My immediate response shocked even me.

"Of course. Absolutely, yes. We all hope for many years of remission. But along with the chemo and radiation, I am going to recommend palliative care."

Palliative? As in, end of life?? I haven't even started the treatment, and you're already telling me I'm going to die???

Clear the Baggage

I thanked the oncologist and left knowing that I had to get multiple opinions. When you're facing adversity, regardless of how grim the situation may seem, you still have options. You can fight like hell for what you believe to be true. Or you can accept the first opinion thrown your way. Now, I'm not the one to tell you which option is best in your situation. Everything is circumstantial. But I will say this. If you're going to live the life you desire, you *must* consider all of your options. My options were fight or die. I chose option number one.

I will not let cancer be my end. I'm not going to become a statistic. I will do everything possible to overcome this. I'm not done with life yet. I've sold myself short. I got stuck in a toxic marriage. If I make it through this, I will make a change. I'll create the future I deserve.

That was the day that little witch left my shoulder. Not going to lie, she still makes an appearance now and then. She doesn't stay long, though. Cancer was a gift. An opportunity to choose a new path. I could've sat idle in life. Instead, I stood up and fought for what I deserved. I wish cancer didn't have to be the witch's eviction notice. If only something less dire could've opened my eyes to the need to put me first no matter what. But with how often I sacrificed my needs for others' demands, I would've found a way to an early death anyway. Depression. Anxiety. Some other life-threatening illness. Staring down The End, I realized I wasn't living the life I should have. I was living my life on autopilot. I was miserable. Unhappy. Exhausted. Either I continued down that path and died, or I didn't. That was the gift—I had a choice. I wanted more time with my kids. I wanted to be financially secure. I wanted more time to experience love. *Real* love. I just wanted to be happy. Even for one second a day.

Let's cut to the chase. After I decided to do whatever I could to get cancer out of my body, I searched all over for a new treatment plan. Did you know it takes four to six weeks to see an oncologist if your cancer isn't terminal? What the hell?! In the meantime, I had a port installed to begin chemotherapy right away. I ordered cold caps to save my hair (they're amazing). I learned how to juice, and I drank so much mushroom tea I started to smell like a mushroom. I lathered myself in essential oils. I prayed. I exercised. And I prepared for whatever they told me to do.

I scheduled consultations with multiple oncologists around the country. They all offered the same treatment plan—chemo, radiation, five years of medication, and luck. That didn't sit well with me. I had to keep searching. Google led me to Banner MD Anderson Cancer Center in Phoenix, Arizona, one of the best health care providers in the nation for women in my situation. I called them up, left my information with the receptionist, and sent all my medical records and paperwork hoping there would be a cancellation. The receptionist told me the next available appointment was in four weeks, but she'd put me on the waiting list in case something opened up sooner. Imagine my disappointment. I settled into the reality of treatment plan B. Then that Friday around 4:00 p.m., I got a call.

"Hi, this is Victoria at MD Anderson. I'm calling because we've had a cancellation. Can you be here at eight o'clock Monday morning for your first appointment?"

"This Monday? Uh, yeah. I mean, yes. I'll be there. That was fast."

"Well, it's very rare we can get someone in so quickly, but cancellations happen."

"I'm glad I got lucky."

"I see you'll be coming from Montana. Do you want a referral to one of our hotel partners? There's a discount for our patients."

"Actually, my parents live in Phoenix. I'll be staying with them."

"Oh, wonderful. You'll need the support."

As soon as I hung up, I got online and bought my plane ticket. My parents picked me up from the airport and drove me to MD Anderson before dawn Monday morning.

When the doctor introduced herself, I knew we were in the right place. She was a beautiful, confident woman with a plan. *She's the one.* The first thing out of her mouth?

"You aren't going to die."

I'm pretty sure my parents and I looked at her like a deer in headlights. As she went over my treatment options, she managed to *not* make a recommendation. Instead, she asked me what approach *I* wanted. That was the first time a doctor had asked me what my thoughts were around my treatment. So I spoke from the heart.

"First, I just feel like I need the surgery. The double. I care so much more about life than I do about my boobs. I want to do whatever I can so I'll *never* go through this again. And second, I need you to be open to my natural approach to medicine. I'm talking about diet, essential oils, herbs, exercise, prayer, meditation . . ."

"That's not a problem. And I completely agree," she said. "We'll find a way to fit you in for a double mastectomy."

They did. I stayed with my parents for eight weeks while my kids stayed in Montana with their dad. Through it all, the little witch never reappeared. Excuses like, *But nobody wants a single mom*, *But I don't deserve a soul mate*, and *But I won't be able to attract a man after a double mastectomy* never touched me. Sure, when you can't do anything for eight weeks, a lot swirls around in your mind while you binge-watch *CSI*. But finally—finally—the self-chatter didn't control me. I made my choice to live for myself. I was a free woman.

I'm grateful I had this experience. Because now I know how to love myself and be true to what matters to me. I don't feel guilty for doing things that make me happy. I did find my soul mate, who brought four wonderful stepkids into my life. Before cancer, I never would've had the confidence to quit my professor job to build a network marketing business so I could have more time with my family. If I hadn't had cancer, I never would've noticed the baggage in my life. It was cancer that made me realize all these adversities, fears, and objections were stopping me from being the person I was supposed to be. They didn't have to hold me back anymore. Cancer gave me a wake-up call, and I answered.

Dare I say thank you, cancer?

SECOND CHANCES

I hope for your sake that my cancer story isn't too relatable. Let's be real. It sucks. However, I do know something is going on in your life that matters to you as much as my health mattered to me; otherwise you wouldn't have picked up this book. You've found yourself at a stage in life where crises are the norm. Maybe it's yours, a loved one's, or a friend's. Whatever the problem, turn it into an opportunity to choose your future. Are you going to take the path less traveled, the path of disruption where you kick excuses in the butt and live life for *you*? Most women don't. They're stuck and too comfortable to change. So was I until I got my diagnosis. Let me tell you, sister—dying isn't comfortable. My choice to clear the baggage gave me a second chance at life. *You* don't have to face an early death to make the same choice.

Take a moment right now and look at your life. You've experienced a lot. Most people our age are married and with older kids. We've gone through at least ten jobs by now. As I said before, now what? You have *so* much more to claim before you call it a life. When we get to our thirties, forties, fifties, and beyond, we can live again—for *ourselves*. But only if we choose it. From this stage onward, it will only get harder to clear the baggage. Because the longer you carry it, the harder it is to dump. So choose wisely. Choose now. Clear the crap. It's OK if you don't know what that looks like yet. That's what this book will help you discover.

For now, I ask you: What are you going to do with your second chance? What adversity in your life can open up a new opportunity? If your little witch says, "But you don't *deserve* a new opportunity," don't listen. Because guess what? Even though you've faced challenges. Even though life broke your heart . . .

You're still here.

CHAPTER 3
YES, YOU DO DESERVE IT

The heaviest weight a woman can carry is the belief she doesn't deserve what she wants. Around the time of my cancer diagnosis, I was contemplating changing my career path. I was running ragged, spending way too much time away from my kids, and barely making ends meet.

When you were a child and dreamed of your future self, none of those realities made your list. But we women are gluttons for punishment. We so easily get sucked into the battle between societal expectations and what we want and deserve out of life. Yes—*what we deserve out of life.*

So why was I questioning what would make me happy, more time with my kids, a successful career, and financial freedom? It's simple. The little witch on my shoulder convinced me I didn't deserve it.

I shouldn't allow myself to have this, went the self-talk. *I don't deserve to be successful. People would view me differently, and I don't want the pressure. I'm a humble girl from Wyoming. My family will be embarrassed. I'll become one of "those" people. I went through all those years of school to be a professor. I already have a successful job. I should be grateful.*

Ah, grateful. What a word. The guilt it makes you feel shuts down your desires. Society tells us to be content with what we have because other people have it worse. *How can I be so ungrateful? I have two great kids, two living parents, and access to the best medical care money can buy. What's wrong with me?! Why can't I just count my blessings?*

You've probably been there, too. Guilt doesn't help you feel gratitude, does it? And that's the real problem here. How many times has someone said to you, "Look at everything you already have. Aren't you grateful?" And better yet, how often have you murmured those exact words to yourself? That's guilt, not gratitude.

THE PROBLEM WITH "GRATITUDE"

Why do we as women feel the need to carry guilt for wanting more of the little things that make us happy? Every woman knows how this gratitude thing goes. We want something, but we don't just want it, we *deserve* it. Then along comes the little witch's voice with lectures about being grateful for what we already have, and we're done. Instead of feeling grateful, we feel awful. Then we're uncomfortable ever wanting more again.

Celebrating your victories cures your guilt and opens your heart to experience genuine gratitude. At our age, we're thinking about retirement and about our future. We're thinking about what life will look like in ten years. Gray hairs and laugh lines are the topic of conversation over wine and gossip with friends. Guess what? We *earned* that gray hair. We *earned* those laugh lines. They show the world all the amazing experiences we've had. They prove that we've lived. We're not stopping. Look at where we've been and what we've done. Celebrate every victory, no matter how small.

How are you celebrating your successes? Every summer I walk out to my garden and see it fuller and greener than the year before. That's a win. It looks amazing, and *I* did it. Your little victory could be taking the time to do those little things that just make you happy. It could be staying at your job for ten years, staying healthy, or eating right. Take a deep breath and look around at your successes. Walk out your front door and look at the home you created. Regardless of whether you rent it or you bought it, it's your home. Look at your family, your friends. Celebrate. Let yourself get into a state of gratitude for what you've accomplished.

I celebrate by writing down a goal in my planner, accomplishing that goal, and checking it off. Achieving goals makes me happy, whether it's paying off a credit card, staying in remission another year, or doubling my annual income. Of course I tell my friends, my husband, and my kids about it. They're my number one cheerleaders.

Whenever work takes me away from my family, my cheerleaders do their thing. Just last week, I had to fly to Atlanta. My son hates it when I'm gone, but my daughter reminded him, "You know, Mom's going to work for us." She's fifteen going on forty.

I'm not perfect when it comes to celebrating my own success. Sometimes I'm a real jerk, and I let my gratitude slip back into guilt. When that happens, I reach out to a girlfriend.

"Hey, Kacie! How are things?"

"Good. I mean, they're OK," I say. "Well, actually, I've gotten into a funk. I snapped at the kids this morning, and I don't even know why. I should be grateful for them."

"*Ugh*, I totally get it. I was tired last week, and I had takeout almost every night. I think I gained five pounds. I'm definitely ready to get back to taking care of myself this week. Let's do ten days of gratitude, OK?"

"Yes." I sigh. "That's exactly what I need."

"Me too. You send me three things you're grateful for every single morning for ten days, and I'll reply back with three things I'm grateful for."

No matter the situation, this little exercise works like a charm. Do it with a friend or simply write it in your planner, which I've found to be equally helpful. It gets me back into the space of living my life for what brings me simple joy. It removes the pressure of scary expectations that come from a space less desirable. Gratitude unlocks our potential to be more and give more. Like a good friend of mine always says, the more you thank life, the more life gives you to be thankful for. Show up in gratitude.

HOPE: THE ANTIDOTE TO MEDIOCRITY

I recently booked a photo shoot to revamp my brand online. The photographer wanted to take a photo of me holding a bottle of essential oil. I grabbed one out of my bag and struck a quick pose. When I looked at the photo, I teared up. The name of the essential oil bottle I had grabbed was "Hope."

Life isn't a coincidence. When I think back over the last several years, even through my divorce and my cancer, I've always had this feeling of hope in my gut. I somehow knew there was more out there for me and that I wasn't going to leave this earth in mediocrity.

What about you and your story? What does mediocrity mean to us as women? What happens when we settle? Mediocrity is the witch incarnate. She's the thief of everything we're meant to do on this earth. Mediocrity keeps us stagnant, safe, and hidden so our true potential never flourishes. How do we break free from its vicious hold on our souls?

Hope. If we don't hope that more is possible, it sure won't be. Hope brought me to where I am today. Hope is at the heart of why I do what I do. I use my story to provide hope to others. The fact that I'm still here experiencing these things is not a coincidence. The people I've met in the last few years, including my new husband (you'll read all the juicy details soon), are in my life because I let myself have hope. I knew I wasn't going to let cancer take me down, and I knew I couldn't die before my children saw what true love looked like. So I kept fighting. I kept celebrating. And I kept hoping.

If you're in a place of despair right now, I urge you to listen to the little hope you have left. You deserve more than settling, and you deserve to celebrate it. You are made for great. Even though the news focuses on the bad and your social media feed would have you believe it, there is so much beauty in this world. I know from experience that the people who come into our lives are here for a reason. Nothing you're experiencing is a coincidence.

When you're in the thick of it, it's tempting to see hope as a fluffy message, but it's so much more than that. It's the root of everything. You are capable of thriving, not just surviving. You *can* live the life you've always wanted. You *can* get to your sweet spot and stay there. You *can* have your convertible and your soul mate, too.

THE MAN WITH THE STELLA: HOW I MET MY SOUL MATE WHILE KICKING CANCER'S BUTT

When you believe you deserve everything you want, you open up a whole new world of possibilities. When I was diagnosed with breast cancer, I made a decision—*I will not die from this anytime soon. Not until I can show my kids what love is supposed to look like.* Their early childhood and upbringing was not ideal. And now that my relationship with their father was over, I was ready for true love. Of course I wanted to find my soul mate, but more than that,

I didn't want my kids to lose their mom and spend the rest of their lives thinking a disrespectful, unhealthy relationship was love. My decision to survive gave me a positive attitude nobody was expecting. My friends kept asking me things like, "How are you so happy? How do you keep going? How do you keep laughing?"

I always had the same reply: "I'm not dying until I can show my kids what it means to be in a loving relationship."

When I finished the first eight weeks of treatment, I had to learn how to live life after a double mastectomy. Nothing—I mean nothing—can prepare you for those emotions. Your body is forever stripped of everything you ever knew. Phantom pains. They're real. Self-doubt. It's brutal. Life goes on. And you always have a friendly reminder that things will never appear the same.

After the surgery, my doctor said to me, "Now that the mastectomy is behind you, it's time to start thinking about what's next. What kind of reconstructive surgery do you want?"

"Uh . . ." I cleared my throat. "I don't know. I really don't care. I'd just as soon get on with my life now, if that's OK."

"You don't want any reconstruction? Most insurance will cover—"

"I'd rather just hold off. Can we talk about it later?"

"Yes. I suppose there's no hurry."

I know. You probably think I'm crazy. Honestly, I hadn't thought about it. As long as I was cancer-free, I was a hundred percent fine with whatever happened. Not enough time had passed for me to care what I looked like. I was still in survival mode. I didn't have a relationship. No one to impress. I'd already accepted I was going to be a marred female with no boobs searching for a man.

Four weeks after my double mastectomy, something shifted. I let go, and I prayed. What my life looked like for the past thirty-eight years was nothing like what the next thirty-eight years would look like. And I simply wasn't sure how I was going to handle it. Single. Scarred. Lonely. Fighting cancer. Who signs up for this? Surely not any sane woman. I remember one night distinctly. Girlfriends. Deep conversation. I asked for the greatest gift in my life. Love.

"I deserve so much more. I *know* I deserve love," I said. For the first time since I found that lump, I was losing it. "And I know that my kids deserve to see their mom happy."

"Oh, Kacie . . ." Jennifer handed me another tissue.

"OK, yes, you deserve love. So what does he look like?" Cathy asked me.

"Who?"

"The man in your head. Your dream guy. The soul mate you deserve."

I sighed. "I *know* I'm going to find him. Obviously I have no freaking clue how or where, but I know I'm going to find him. For God's sake, my heart and arms are wide open. What better way to find my soul mate?"

Cathy nodded. "I agree. But you're dodging the question. What's he like?"

"He makes me laugh," I said. "He's successful in his career. Maybe he has crazy hair. He likes to dance. He'll take me on weekend trips to the city, and we'll go to concerts and eat yummy food on the street. And we'll travel together in a convertible." I could almost feel his presence. Because it was at this moment I began to manifest my soul mate (Friends, if you aren't manifesting things in your life, it's time you do.).

I boarded a plane the next morning and headed to my post-op appointment. In the world of cancers and hospitals, nothing changes. The smell stays the same. The people look the same. The same sadness permeates the space. And "hope" isn't a word spoken much. Cancer sucks. That phrase should not be taken lightly. Yet on that day, June 24, 2013, my belief shifted. Cancer somehow became my gift.

"Hello, Kacie. How are you?" My doctor greeted me in the exam room with a huge hug.

"Depends," I said. "Is the cancer gone?"

She smiled. "We don't get to say this often, but I can confidently say it to you now. We think we've cured you. All the tests came back negative, and your numbers look great. You'll still need to come in for tests regularly for the next year, but I'd say it's time you start living your life again."

A long overdue smile crept over my face. *Start living my life again. That's my go-ahead*, I thought. *I got permission from the doctor. It's time I start doing what I'm meant to be doing in my life.*

I walked out of the office and drove my rental car to the Phoenix airport. After I checked in, I still had an hour before boarding, so I headed to the one and only restaurant at the Delta gate—a little Mexican place, with the intent to start exploring options for my second chance at life. I sat down at the bar. *You know what? I'm going to have a beer. I'm going to celebrate my life and what I have ahead of me.*

As I sat on the barstool sipping my overpriced (and delicious) beverage, I opened a group text to my girlfriends.

The Sweet Spot

Doctor says I'm cured. Everything looks great. What should we do first? I hit send. *So I guess I get to live my life now*, I added. *Now I get to find my man.*

"Hey," a deep voice said behind me. "Is the seat next to you taken?"

I turned around. Standing not three feet behind me was the man I had told my girlfriends about. He wore a button-up shirt, dress pants, and these hot Italian leather shoes. *Classy. Successful. Cute.* The rush of energy caught me off guard. I'd always been faithful to my then-husband, and I hadn't even looked at another guy in twenty years. I felt like I was sixteen years old again.

I glanced over my shoulder at all the open seats.

"No, it's not taken."

He smiled, shoved his luggage under the bar, and sat down next to me.

Oh my gosh, I texted my girlfriends. *Hot guy just sat down next to me. Literally right next to me. Panic mode! What should I do?*

He asked the bartender for a Pabst Blue Ribbon.

Flirt with him!!! my friend Callie texted back.

It's been twenty-some years since I flirted. But whatever, I'll give it a try.

"You can't order a PBR dressed like that," I said.

He looked me up and down. "You can't be dressed like that in Arizona."

I glanced down at my long skirt and fleece jacket. Outside, it was one hundred and twenty degrees. In July, some flights out of Phoenix can't take off because it's too hot. The guy had a point.

"I have an excuse." I shrugged. "I got a really bad boob job." I'm not kidding. That was my reply. *Ugh*.

He laughed awkwardly. "Huh," he said and pulled his laptop out of his leather satchel.

I updated my girlfriends. *OK, this is the epic fail of flirting. He totally thinks I'm a weirdo. Here I am telling a hot guy I got a bad boob job.*

He finished his first beer and waved at the bartender. "I'll take a Stella and my check, please," he added.

Stella—I always loved that name.

Oh my gosh, I typed. *He's making me crazy. He's so cute.*

Well, flash him! Jennifer texted back.

I laughed out loud. Hot guy beside me jumped.

I turned bright red. My then-husband had told me that my "cackle" was "the most annoying noise" he'd ever heard.

"Oh my gosh. I'm so sorry I startled you," I mumbled. "One of my girlfriends just sent me this hilarious text . . ."

He shut his computer and turned to face me. "Don't apologize. Your laugh is contagious." He smiled. "I love it. Please never stop."

OK, this is freaking magical, I thought.

"Mike," he said, extending his hand.

"Hi." I laughed again and took it. "I'm Kacie."

He asked me what I did. I asked him what he did. You know, casual questions. Nothing too personal. Or memorable. At least at the time.

The bartender brought our checks just as I heard the boarding announcement for my flight.

"That's me," I said, pointing to my gate. My heart was beating so fast I worried he'd notice.

"Hey, me too. Can I walk with you?"

"Sure."

"You know, Kacie," Mike said as we got up to leave. "I'm not done with you. We're both on this flight to Salt Lake City. Would you mind having dinner with me in Salt Lake? I have an hour layover before my flight to Reno. Usually I stay at my Park City home, but I've got a meeting in Nevada—"

"Yes. Oh yes. Yes. Oddly enough, I have an hour layover before my flight to Bozeman."

"Great."

We walked out together and remained side by side until we boarded. We made small talk, and that was it.

"Well, have a nice flight," I said as I left Mike in business class.

"Thanks, you too. See you at dinner." He smiled again.

When we open ourselves up to the opportunities we deserve, we attract them—and more. I must have been radiating open energy to the masses that day, because as I approached my seat, the elderly man sitting next to mine stood.

"I've been dreaming about you," he said.

What a weird day. First, I'm declared cancer-free, then a hot guy asks me out, and now an eighty-five-year-old man is telling me he's dreaming about me. What's next?

I didn't say anything as I sat down. So he repeated himself.

"I've been dreaming about you because you're my angel."

Is this guy off his meds? Or does he actually need something from me? Maybe I should be open-minded. Something about him looks strangely familiar.

"I'm Luis," he continued. "I'm not in the best of health. I'm . . . struggling."

"I'm sorry to hear that." I tried to put my finger on who he reminded me of. "Have you seen a doctor?"

"Not yet. I don't have insurance. Hard to get in and see someone. I don't think I could afford it anyway."

Then it hit me. His eyes showed he'd been crying. His voice sounded weak. He reminded me . . . of *me*. Right before I got my diagnosis. When my life was falling apart and I thought it couldn't get any worse. Did this man have cancer, too? Or was that beer hitting me just now?

"I sell essential oils," I said. "If I give you a free oil sample, would you use it?"

"Yes. Absolutely. I'll try anything that doesn't come from a doctor."

I reached into my purse and gave him a small bottle. Frankincense.

"Here. Put one drop under your tongue every day. It won't taste good, but I think it will help you feel better."

He smiled at me. "Thank you. I will." He opened the bottle and held it up to his face. "Like this?" He stuck out his tongue.

"Yep, you've got it. Just tilt the bottle up and let it drop under your tongue."

He did as I said and then wrinkled his nose. "Bleh. You were right about the taste."

I smiled. "I warned you."

"Well, I've had worse." He chuckled. "If it helped me, I'd drink the whole bottle."

"Yeah, don't do that."

"Yes, ma'am. Thank you again."

We sat in silence for a few minutes.

"I have a son," Luis said. "I'm going to see him in Utah. It's been too long. He's about your age. Very successful."

Oh boy. Here we go. He's going to set me up with his son.

"I'm not really looking for—"

"Oh, I wasn't trying to play matchmaker," he said. "I just wanted you to know where I was going, angel."

"OK." I smiled.

We didn't say much to each other for the rest of the flight. Once I peeked over at Luis and saw him taking these deep, calm breaths—like he hadn't a care in the world. Peaceful. I'll never forget his face.

When the plane landed, Luis and I walked out together. I could see Mike up ahead waiting for me at the gate. Luis turned to me, wrapped his arms around me, and gave me a huge kiss.

"Let me give you my card." I reached into my bag. "Please feel free to reach out."

"Thank you," Luis said. "My angel." And he disappeared into the crowd of passengers shuffling up to the gate.

"Wow," Mike said when I caught up. "I guess I have some competition. You're attracting everyone today."

Luis reached out to me the next week. He said that he'd gone to urgent care because he kept throwing up blood. They'd sent him to the hospital, where he was diagnosed with stage four colon cancer. He had only weeks to live.

"I wanted to let you know, and to thank you," he told me when we spoke on the phone. "I'm still using that oil, and maybe it's in my head, but when I take it, I feel better about my life."

I don't know what I did for Luis. Maybe he needed a genuine connection with another human being. Maybe he needed to know what love looked like before he passed—even for a few moments.

Back at the Salt Lake City airport, Mike and I walked to a restaurant near the gate of my next flight. We sat in the dim back corner. He ordered a bottle of Silver Oak—the priciest on the menu.

"This is one of my favorite wines. I would love to share it with you," he said.

Man, this guy doesn't mess around. Wait until the girls hear about this.

From there, we gave our best attempt at small talk. It was rough.

"What kind of music do you like?"

I panicked. What if I told him I liked Shania Twain and he hated country? Should I lie?

"I dunno," I said, looking down. "I like everything, really."

"OK. What's your baggage like? You mentioned divorce and a boob job, so you must have some serious stuff in your bag."

"Um . . ."

I couldn't tell him I had cancer. You don't come out and say that on your first—whatever this thing was we were doing. A date?

After forty-five minutes of small talk, I couldn't tell if I knew him any better.

When it was time to catch our flights, Mike took care of the check. *He's hot* and *a gentleman*. Then as we both stood up, he bent over and kissed me on my cheek. I leaned in. His lips took my breath away. Literally. I gasped. I couldn't breathe. I honestly thought I was going to pass out.

"Are you OK?" Mike chuckled.

"I don't think so."

He laughed, I laughed. Then we exchanged business cards.

"I think we should make something clear between us," Mike said. "We're both respectable individuals. I think we need to clean up our houses before we have another conversation, if you know what I mean."

"I totally agree," I said.

"I look forward to seeing more of you, Kacie."

Two weeks went by. No calls, no texts. I started to forget what Mike's smile looked like. How his voice sounded. Even what color his hair was. But I didn't forget how he made me feel.

Around that two-week mark, I took my kiddos to see Justin Bieber in concert in Denver. Before the long drive, I pulled up to Callie's house to carpool with her and her daughter. My kids discussed possible set lists while we waited. I took out my phone, opened my email, and started typing. Leave it to Bieber to bring out the courage in me.

Dear Mike,

I don't know why I'm sending this to you. Maybe it's because you're so hot. But I feel inclined to answer your questions because I want you to know that I actually am human, that I do have a clue, and that I do have a life.

Number one: What kind of music do you like? I love country and classic rock. Shania Twain is in my CD player as we speak.

Number two: What's your baggage? Well, I had cancer. The day we met, I got the news that I was officially in remission. And I'm going through a divorce, as you know.

I know our paths will probably never cross unless we make a plan to see each other again. But I wanted you to know my real answers.

He replied back before Callie and her daughter showed.

Kacie,

I don't know what it is about you, but you've got me. You've got me so fascinated. I'm so intrigued to know more about you. The next time you're in Phoenix, reach out to me because I have clients there. Maybe we can go and have coffee.

That started six weeks of emails back and forth. Then two days before my next appointment at MD Anderson, I sent him a quick message.

Hey, I have to be in Arizona on Friday. Wanna get that coffee?

Man, Mike wrote. *I don't know if I can pull that off on such short notice.*

Oh. I just wanted to see you.

I want to see you, too. Maybe our lives will cross paths again soon. I don't know what you did to me, but I appreciate it.

I didn't respond. What was I supposed to say? I was so bummed.

Four hours later, Mike wrote me again.

Change of plans. I actually do need to go to Arizona for a meeting. Are we back on?

I tried to control my excitement.

OK, awesome, I wrote back. *When do you want to meet?*

I'm going to stay at the Westin. My business will pay for the room. I was wondering if you'd like to share with me and save some money.

I think my heart stopped. The last six weeks gave me plenty of time to "clean up my house." No need to tell him I could stay with my parents.

Heck, yes.

Heck, yes? he replied back.

Heck, yes, I wrote again. *Oh my gosh, what are we doing? Should we be doing this?*

Yes, we should be doing this, he wrote.

That Thursday morning, we both hopped on a plane and met at the Salt Lake City airport before our flight together to Phoenix. We had a two-hour layover. When I got off the plane, I watched him give me a once-over. I was wearing a cute sundress and heels. Not my normal casual attire, but hey, new beginnings, new comfort zone.

We hung out at the airport for two hours and enjoyed a goofy conversation. Our attraction to each other was out of control. When we checked into our room at the Westin in Phoenix, I grabbed his arm.

"If you're going to be with me, you have to understand something."

I stood in front of him and unbuttoned my shirt. My fresh scars were still red.

"You're beautiful," Mike said with the softest look in his eyes.

At that moment, I knew he was going to be in my life forever.

The next morning, we shared a kiss before leaving for the day in our respective rental cars. We agreed to meet up for dinner. I headed to my doctor's appointment and Mike to his meeting.

I pulled into the MD Anderson parking lot. Even now, it was emotional. The last couple of appointments, I hadn't asked my parents to join me. These were basic checkups, so I didn't want to bother them after all they had previously done. It was just me.

My phone rang as I put the car in park.

"Where are you?" Mike asked.

"I'm about to go into my doctor's appointment," I said. "Why?"

"Give me two minutes. I moved my meeting. I'm coming with you. There will never be another day that you go to a doctor's appointment alone."

I was still wiping tears off my face when he parked in the space next to mine. He got out of his car and hugged me.

"Let's go," Mike said, and we walked in together.

With all the follow-up tests, my appointment that day was five hours long. Over those five hours, Mike listened with me to every possible relapse scenario. He heard about every lifestyle change I needed to make to survive and remain cancer-free. From that day forward, Mike held my hand through every single appointment.

As soon as I saw his face in the parking lot, I knew Mike was my soul mate. If you got his take on this story, he'd say the same thing. We knew we were going to be in each other's lives forever. That's the power of being open to what you deserve—amazing things happen. When you stop listening to that little witch on your shoulder telling you what you don't deserve, you can reach your sweet spot. And when you get there, you may just find your soul mate.

In the summer of 2019, Mike and I celebrated four years of marriage. I look at where I am today, and I know he's a big part of why I'm a survivor. He fulfilled my desire to show my kids what love looked like before I left this earth. And now there's no way I'm giving up on life. Mike made me a fighter. He completes me. We are each other's greatest victory. And for that, I will always be grateful.

Soon after we got married, we adopted a Great Dane.

We named her Stella.

CHAPTER 4
YES, YOU CAN FEEL FEAR AND ACT ANYWAY

Fear is a nasty beast.

What if people think I'm a bad mom for taking a bath once a week? What if my spouse and kids don't like me taking one night a week to build a direct sales business? What if I'm not flexible enough for the yoga class I've always wanted to take and I look stupid?

That little witch whispers these what-ifs into our head, and before you know it, our fears become excuses. We give up what makes us happy, and we're convinced we've got a good reason to do so. You'd think the little witch would be happy just slapping down the little things. Nope. She goes after the big dreams, too. Fear predicts the worst-case scenario about everything, slaps down our confidence, and stops us from showing up as our best self.

Just like that, a beautiful opportunity turns into an ugly monster. Fear convinces us we'll lose what we already have, so we'd better not upset the status quo. Most of our fears lie in change, whether it's starting a business, ending a toxic relationship, or buying a new house. When we leave our safe little comfort zone, we don't have complete control anymore. Lack of control is *scary*. So fear tells us we best not step beyond the space we're living in. Let's stay comfortable. Stay complacent. Whatever. It's easier to stay miserable than risk screwing up, falling flat, and making things worse. Or so fear tells us.

Well, guess what, friend? When you cling to what feels safe, you know what happens? You get stuck. Your energy stops flowing in a positive and productive way. Why not put that energy to use before it's gone? Embrace your sweet spot and everything in it. But listen to fear and you flee the good life. You make up excuses, then get people around you to support your fear. It's a terrible cycle. And we've all been there. You're not alone. It's not your fault you've been listening to the little witch. But it ends now—because I'm going to help you snap out of it. I'm your splash of cold water, your kick in the pants, and your support system all in one.

MAKE FEAR YOUR MENTOR

In a recent coaching call, I was asked the simple question, "What do you want?" I rattled off my passion for supporting women in their business, increasing my capacity to serve, becoming a more powerful influencer, breaking free from my small-time thinking, being a better mom, spending more time with Mike, and growing a massive garden. The only problem was at the end of my personal sharing moment, I ended with the words, "I don't know." Yes, juicy goodness turned to gasping for breath. The other end went silent, and I knew I had said the dreaded words that gave fear permission. The witch whispered in my ear. *You don't deserve this. You aren't capable of coaching these women. You aren't smart enough. You can't manage a business and family. And social media . . . oh boy, it'll eat your lunch.*

And for a split second, I believed those voices. Then the reality police smacked me. OK, that's an exaggeration. It was my coach. And she didn't physically smack me. She simply said, "Kacie, can I be real and raw with you? Why are you so afraid?"

Her words struck me. I mean, they really struck me. Why was I so afraid of becoming the person I was meant to be? What was holding me back from showing up in a space I was completely ready to embrace? It came down to one word—change. The fear of change and disruption stopped me dead in my tracks.

How did I get over my fear of disrupting the status quo in my business and my family? Well, I didn't pretend away those fears. You can't ignore fear, I've realized. In fact, I don't believe it's even possible to make fear go away. You probably agree with me there. You know what else I realized? *If you can't beat fear, join it.* What? Nobody says that. But I say let's *partner* with fear. Let's turn fear into a motivational speaker.

I have yet to read a book that says it's possible to use your fear to your advantage. Yet it totally is. When we embrace our fear instead of hiding from it, the little witch can't take us by surprise. Whether you want to start a side business, move to another state, go on an adventure of a lifetime, or change the family schedule, *you should be scared.* And if you're not, you're more confident than any other woman I know.

Here's the thing. What's the worst thing that can happen? You try something new and it doesn't work exactly like you plan. You disrupt your family schedule and for a month they are uncomfortable. You nurture your relationships and things get better. At the end of the day, no matter how things end up, change equals growth and growth equals goodness.

From now on, friend, you are going to turn that fear into excitement. It's not that far of a jump—the two feelings are already so similar. The butterflies in your stomach before a first kiss, the worry you'll run smack into the wall at a job interview. Anytime you're up against something foreign or uncomfortable, you get that same feeling. Excitement. Panic. It's all the same. If the little witch fills your head with horrors, create a plan of action around them to prevent them from happening. In other words, fear can open a door that leads right to your sweet spot. The question is, will you choose to walk through it?

If you don't, you'll stay stuck. You'll never make the little things that just make you happy part of your everyday life. But if you step up and step through, the *opposite* of fear happens. And that, my friend, is a little thing called courage.

DO THIS TO COUNTERACT FEAR

When I left my professor job, I'd been running my network marketing business on the side for almost a year. I'd decided that if I wanted to upgrade my paycheck and spend more time with my kiddos, I should try this direct sales thing. When I reframed my fear of running a business into excitement, my business blew up bigger than I imagined. I stopped teaching. One decision disrupted everything—my income, my routine, my attitude, my relationship. For two years, everyone around me thought I was nuts. At times, I thought I was a little crazy, too. But in my heart, I knew this business was my only option, so I took it.

A lot easier said than done, right? Here's how I gathered the courage to quit teaching—I tested my fear. Before I typed the first word of that letter of resignation, I weighed my current situation against those little things that just make me happy. Comfort zone versus sweet spot. I just wanted control over my situation . . . someone to appreciate my hard work . . . a paycheck I could control.

I also got clear on what I *didn't* want in my life. I didn't want my schedule tied to someone else's. I didn't want to be away from my kids when they needed me. I didn't want to be stressed out and exhausted all the time. Of course I was terrified to jump into a new adventure. Fear paralyzes you if you don't move fast. That's why I didn't prolong my decision. I compared my current situation to a hopeful future. I thought about who and what I would disrupt if I went full-time into my business. Disruption was the path for me.

I bet it is for you, too. Disruption is how successful people got to where they are. What if you stepped toward fear, disrupted your status quo, and got what you wanted out of life? What would happen if you spent more time with your spouse? What's the *worst* that could happen? How could doing any of these things have any result other than positive?

If I can come up with one truly negative thing about something I want to do, I'm probably not going to do it. Take changing the entire household menu, getting everyone on a set schedule, or turning off tech gadgets at a certain time. That's disruption. And it's worth it. So don't make a pros and cons list about what you know in your heart you need to do. That's how you procrastinate your way into inaction. Think about the results of your disruption. Nothing to fear here. Odds are, I probably can't come up with one negative response to eating healthy, spending more time with my girlfriends, or becoming successful. Why stir up negative energy in the first place?

When you're confident about the end result of your disruption, you don't worry that you might get judged or look stupid. Newsflash: it doesn't matter what people say, how they think you look, or if people believe you're playing the right role. *Am I doing everything my friends expect me to do at this moment?* Yeah . . . what a terrible way to live. This is *your* life, not theirs. The path of disruption always leads you into the spotlight. Anytime someone turns fear into fuel, they're going to get noticed. I've been rolling as an introvert most of my life, and I can't avoid the spotlight. But the last thing I'm going to do is cave to expectations.

The most valuable thing a woman can do is stay true to her beliefs and keep living the life that makes her happy. Likewise, you should expect drama from all the wrong people when you turn fear into excitement. Even something as small as going to bed an hour early so you can get up and enjoy your morning coffee in peace has its fair share of detractors. Your spouse, your kids, your girlfriends, whoever. So what? Do it anyway.

The blowback is *never* as bad as you expect. I learned that from my daughter. After six months of begging and pleading, she wore me down. When she turned fourteen, I took her to get her nose pierced. There's only so much the mother of a teenager can say no to. Yes, I'm not perfect. I gave in. Anyway, I kept my mouth shut, but I'll tell you now . . . that nose ring the jewelry store gave her looked horrible. I felt embarrassed for her sake on the walk back to our car. You know what she was doing in the meantime? Bouncing around, taking a hundred and twenty selfies, and blowing up social media. No grown woman could pull off that confidence. For her, the spotlight with all its opinions and expectations was the right place to be. She must've known that when she got a prettier nose ring (which she did), her piercing would look amazing (and I'll admit, it does).

My teenage daughter was OK with being uncomfortable. An adult would've gone around worrying. *Does it look good? Is it OK? What will people think? Should I post a picture or just take it out right now?* That's what being in the spotlight does—it causes discomfort. But in the end, we grow. We make a change, we stick with it, and we get confidence in return.

WHEN FEAR WAS RIGHT

Is feeling afraid and acting anyway always this easy? No. Life isn't always sunshine, rainbows, and moscato. Every woman at our stage of life has experienced her unfair share of failures and screwups. Look at me. Growing up, I was never the best at anything. I had crappy boyfriends, my first marriage sucked, and I got a 1.3 GPA my first year in college. I pretty much failed, failed, and failed. Maybe you carry with you the shame of dead dreams even today.

Time to let 'em go, sister. If you can honestly tell me that you tried, that you did everything you told yourself you would do, then that's a victory no matter the outcome. View those experiences as deposits into a success account. The next time you want to "buy in" to your sweet spot—start a side business, take golf lessons, journal every day—all you have to do is "cash out." Every experience, even the so-called failures, is a resource you can use to achieve your heart's desire this time around.

How so? Experience lets you know ahead of time which fears will materialize and which won't. Now you can plan accordingly. Maybe you tried entrepreneurship in your early twenties, and it was just the worst. Now in your forties, you're realizing you need control over your paycheck if you're going to have the retirement you and your spouse always talk about. Friend, that sweet spot won't happen if you don't disrupt your career. So, what went wrong twenty years ago? Poor product? No support? Crappy sales technique? If you can look back on that experience and identify the problems, you can plan for them when they turn up again. The same goes for a bad first marriage, a crappy ex-girlfriend, or a not-so-flattering bob haircut. You now have a second chance to try a little thing that will make you happy, and you're in a better position to succeed than ever before.

Remember my dream of traveling in my convertible? I gave it up because I was broke for so many years. When I dealt with cancer, went through divorce, and faced losing it all, enjoying my fantasy car with my soul mate was, well, a fantasy. No way from here to there, I believed at the time. I came out of the crisis with the courage and the plan to take back my dream. My business gave me a clearer vision of how exactly to achieve that dream. Was I scared? You bet. Did that stop me? No freaking way. I looked at what went wrong the first time around and mapped a detour around my worst-case scenario. Then all I had to do was stay committed and follow what I knew in my heart would make me happy. Turns out my second time around was my best time around. Yours can be, too.

CHAPTER 5
FOREVER ENOUGH

"But I don't have enough _____."

Fill in the blank. Yours may be time, energy, motivation, or all three. I totally get it, sister. I know you feel like you don't have enough for the little things that just make you happy. When it's 9:00 p.m. and the kids are finally in bed, it's so easy to postpone running that bath or making that cup of tea. You feel guilted into washing the dishes piling up, then you collapse on the sofa to mindlessly scroll social media until you drag yourself to bed at eleven. But let me ask you—does that make you happy?

Now let's get serious here. When's the last time you scheduled time for yourself? Don't get me wrong—I get it. It's hard to find time and energy for self-care or even simply showering at times. When we see sparkling clean houses and perfectly behaved kids on TV, we feel like we're not doing enough. You *can* change that mindset. And you *can* stop making excuses for not doing the little things that just make you happy. Now, I'm not asking you to all of a sudden spend eight hours on yourself every day. What I am asking you to do is shift your priorities. And guess what? You already know how to do that. It's an almost magical ability women have—if something is important, we *find* the time. We *work up* the energy. And we get it done.

Unfortunately, self-care often also falls into the category of "I really should do it, but I never get around to it." I'll be honest—that's what I said for a long time. It wasn't until my diagnosis that I got intentional about finding a space for my happy place. After making a few shifts (which I will teach you to do), I decided to never go back to the old way of depleting my time and energy on everyone else. Now my self-care is nonnegotiable. Does that mean it was easy? Oh my, hell no. It was hard to integrate "me" time into my everyday life. I'll tell you why.

As women, we're not taught to find the time and energy for self-care without feeling selfish. That's why drinking wine in a bubble bath feels like such a dang chore. You're sitting there in the tub thinking about a hundred other things you could be doing. *Is this even worth it?!* you think. How are you supposed to get to your sweet spot when you can't even enjoy something sweet for thirty minutes?

I'm here to tell you—self-care is always worth it. Multiple times a week, I close the bathroom door, light a few candles, fill the tub up, and grab a book. The first few times I found myself worrying about what was happening outside the door. Was my daughter strangling my son? Dog pooping in the hall? Oven left on? After a few weeks of forcing myself to turn on that faucet, something changed. I started *enjoying* myself. I was in a better mood when I got out. I felt more relaxed—batteries recharged. That's when I realized my self-care was anything but selfish. Could I spend that time with my family? Technically, yes. But after a few weeks of skipping my little happy place, I'd feel drained and crave a timeout from life. When I emerge from my bath, I'm a cheerful wife and mother. Time and energy invested in me pays off for everyone.

I want that for you, too. So let's take away the "not enough" excuse and shut that little witch up. The truth is you *can* find the time, and you *do* have the energy. It may not feel like it. Maybe you're even checking the clock right now because you feel guilty about reading this book instead of baking muffins for the church bake sale. That's OK. You do have enough for what matters, and I'm going to help you find it.

A GUILT-FREE GUIDE TO SELF-CARE

Here are a few little tricks that help me take back my time and protect my energy so I can enjoy my sweet spot guilt-free.

START SPONTANEOUSLY

I've heard so many opinions on when the best time for self-care is.

Set your alarm thirty minutes earlier every morning so you can meditate before the kids wake up.

Get ready for bed an hour early and take a bath before bed.

Eat lunch at your desk so you can get your hair done or get a massage on your lunch hour.

Guess what? They're all wrong. When you're taking baby steps to your sweet spot, scheduling a rigid time to practice self-care will only make you more stressed.

I can just imagine thinking, *OK, it's six in the morning. I must sit and meditate right now before I get my kids up, make sure my son is showered, and prepare lunches all before eight.* There is no need to put all that pressure on yourself. Forcing yourself to relax is an oxymoron—it's stressful and it doesn't work.

If you're new at this self-care thing, be flexible. "Me time" doesn't have to be at a certain time of day or for a certain length of time. There are so many little things you can implement immediately into your life when it comes to self-care. You can start by reading an amazing book. Go on a walk with your spouse or friend. You can pick up the phone and ask that girlfriend you've been meaning to catch up with to join you for a lunch date. Whatever makes you smile, you *can* make it happen. And you don't have to do it all at once. I probably have about fifteen self-care moments a day. Do they all last thirty minutes? No way. For me, self-care is anything that connects me with what I love. Whether that's gardening, heading out to the chicken coop, enjoying a sunset on the deck, loving on my dogs, or having sweet conversations with my daughter.

Self-care doesn't have to be just about us or just for us. Sure, alone time is great. But I've had some of my favorite self-care moments with my family. When I'm gardening, I call my kids out to help. When I'm brushing the horses, I chat with my husband. If you find something you love to do, don't be afraid that inviting those you love to do it with you will negate your self-care time. Whoever I'm with and wherever I am, I can take a deep breath and savor the moment.

See? Self-care can be flexible. It can be whatever you want it to be. Create small pockets of time for yourself throughout your day, and before you know it, you'll start to feel good about feeling good. Then you'll be ready to time block.

TIME BLOCK

As a mother and a business owner, I've figured out something about myself—if I have a plan, I can do anything. I know, I know. Having a plan sounds cliché, but it's what successful people do. I've spent thousands of dollars on health, business, and life coaches. They all ask the same thing: *What do you want, and what's your plan to get it?*

The day I started my business, I hatched a plan for myself. *In two years, if I'm making $5,000 a month, I'll keep doing it. If I'm not, then I'm getting out.*

Whenever I meet like-minded business owners, I go right to asking about their business plan.

"You're not happy with your life. I get it. So what's your plan to change things? What have you tried that hasn't worked? What do your weekly activities look like? What's on your schedule right now?"

Most of the time, they have nothing. No ideas, no game plan, no to-do list. They can't even tell me what they *did* try because they haven't tried anything. *Hello . . . It's no wonder you're not succeeding, sister. You can't just sit around expecting things to change on their own. You have to change them. You've got to get a plan together, block off time on your schedule to work on that plan, and follow through.*

What goes for building a successful business goes for finding the time and energy to do something for yourself. To get something done, block off a time for it, whether that's a manicure or a business lunch. You can be flexible and have a schedule at the same time. I know how hard it is to remember the little things, especially when they don't involve anyone else. That's why I put everything on my calendar. Once I write it down or type it into my phone, I don't have to think about it anymore. If it's on my calendar, it gets done, period. I treat every activity like a meeting so nothing can get scheduled over it. It doesn't matter what it is or what comes up. If my business partner calls while I'm exercising, they can wait. I don't need to answer and tell them what I'm doing first. My time is already blocked off for someone else (me).

I used to brain dump a list of "goals" for myself every Monday morning. What made it onto my list? Anything and everything that came into my head. Clean out the litter box, mail packages, schedule a dentist appointment, do laundry, organize kitchen cabinets. You name it, it was on my list. Then I spent the rest of the week feeling overwhelmed, worrying about checking things off. On Friday afternoon, sometimes I hadn't accomplished anything from that week's list—or the previous week's. Needless to say, this strategy didn't last long.

Now, instead of twenty little meaningless goals, I focus on one or two big work projects a week. Guess what? I treat my sweet spot the same way. I know I'm not going to make myself a tasty green smoothie, watch a movie, go shoe shopping, and take an hour-long walk every day. So I focus on what I *can* do that I know will just make me happy. My morning workout, my essential oils, hiking, baking with my family—they're all on my schedule so I literally can't miss them.

When you dedicate time in your schedule to these little things that just make you happy, they become part of your day-to-day life. Habits. Once you get used to this routine, you don't think about rescheduling that bubble bath or skipping a week altogether. I know that if I wake up late, my whole day feels behind. So I've started blocking out time every morning until 10:00 a.m. for *me*. What will you find on my schedule? I work out, check in with my husband, journal, see the kids off, and have a shower before stepping into my office. That same time block is in my calendar every weekday. This creates momentum and allows me to fit in some self-care before I jump into work.

Maybe you're not a morning person. That's OK. Try blocking off time in the evening or even in the middle of the day. It doesn't matter what you do or when you do it. All that matters is that you do it. I know it seems daunting at first to schedule regular time for yourself. Remember, baby steps. First, try scheduling one thing for yourself every week. It doesn't have to be the same thing or at the same time. See what time of day is easiest for you to get some alone time. Then once you feel more comfortable, try scheduling something for yourself every day. Maybe a workout. Maybe an hour to read a chapter from your favorite book. Maybe catching a movie with the whole family. Little by little, you'll develop a daily self-care routine just like I have. Our family sticks to a pretty regular schedule at my house. Monday nights I dedicate to my business. Every Tuesday and Wednesday night is set aside for kids' projects, including sports. Thursdays I tackle a project around the house. Friday night is date night. By scheduling these routines in advance, we've worked self-care into the family schedule. We know what to expect for the week, and we never have to remember to make time for each other.

No matter how tired you are or how overwhelmed you feel, time blocking works for everyone. So what is it you want to do? What would make you happy? Being intimate with your spouse? Getting up early for fresh coffee in peace? Starting your own business? Get it on your schedule and you'll lock in the time and energy you need to make it happen.

How much do you want what you want? Seriously. For me, I was passionate enough about changing my financial situation that I was going to do it no matter what. Whatever I could do to make that happen was getting scheduled into my planner. I was going to work it in around teaching forty hours a week at the university. And if I was going to sell people on self-love, then I had to put thirty minutes of self-love into my calendar every day. I didn't think I had time for that, but I put it in there anyway because

I believe in practicing what I preach. They don't teach you this stuff in school.

They should.

JOURNAL WITH GRATITUDE

Each day, I think of three to five things I'm thankful for and write about them in my planner—my version of a journal. They can be the clothes on my back, our beautiful home, or my second chance at life.

I started doing this exercise for self-reflection, but it didn't take long for me to realize it blew up my energy level. Journaling about my family, the amazing women in my life, everything I'm so unbelievably lucky to have, and my life-changing essential oils makes me feel like I've had a triple espresso.

I don't know about this journaling thing, Kacie. I tried to keep a journal once or twice. Half the time I forgot about it, and when I remembered, I couldn't think of anything to write.

I get it, sister. First of all, don't put so much pressure on yourself. Whether you write a sentence or a page, you've succeeded. This shouldn't take more than five or ten minutes. It isn't a diary. Focus on what you're grateful for, not what you did with your girlfriends last weekend. Then—you guessed it—put it on your schedule so you make sure to do it again.

HIRE IT OUT

It may be up to you to make sure things get done around the house, but it's not your responsibility to do everything—work, cook, clean, you name it. If you don't want to do X, hire it out. For me, my cleaning ladies are nonnegotiable. I told Mike that no matter what our budget is, I am *not* giving up my cleaning ladies because (a) they're amazing, and (b) I don't want to spend my weekend scrubbing toilets when I could be hanging out with him and the kiddos.

If you can't afford daily gourmet meals or a weekly house cleaning right now, save a little of every paycheck for a monthly dinner special or a once-a-quarter deep clean. (In the meantime, check out my book *The Essentials* and learn how to start a profitable business so you can afford those daily meals and weekly cleanings.) It's OK to buy our time back!

GET CREATIVE

For me, self-care is my bath, my garden, and my morning routine. But for someone else, gardening might feel like a chore. There are so many forms of self-care you can try. If you don't love reading, I'm not going to recommend you become a bookworm. Get creative with what you consider self-care. It doesn't have to be a certain thing. It's personal—that's why I often refer to it as personal development.

If you like podcasts, turn one on while you're painting your nails. If you love music, create an amazing playlist.

The Sweet Spot

Notice what you're doing when you feel totally at peace and connected with yourself. Maybe it's doing a home improvement project, playing with your dog, or going to a yoga class. No matter what it is, claim that time or activity as your self-care and schedule more of it. Find what feeds your soul and do more of that. Because ultimately, that's where you want to put your time and energy.

Even in chaotic moments, there are still opportunities to take care of yourself. By picking things you know you love doing, you'll be able to integrate self-care into your day-to-day routine. When you know what to do, put it on your schedule so you'll know when to do it. Then you won't have to worry about making time and finding energy for self-care—because it's already happening.

CHAPTER 6
THE SURPRISING TRUTH ABOUT EXPECTATIONS

We often don't get what we want because we don't have clear expectations about what it takes to get it. Why? Because we take that little witch at her word when she says, "But you don't have the skills to make that happen." Even when everyone around us knows that's not true.

The little witch is also to blame when we do the exact opposite. We go blundering into something with unrealistic expectations, and the little witch keeps her mouth shut so she can enjoy our misery later. It's not fair. We can cry about it, or we can overcome the mistakes and move on. I choose the latter. It's only natural—women are *made* to overcome.

When we are faced with an obstacle, we find a way around it. At sixteen, Mike's daughter came to us asking for help with applying to colleges. In her mind, the conversation was simple.

"I want to ski race at this college. Then become a successful event planner. Get married and start a family. Move by my sisters. And live happily ever after."

All seems reasonable from the mouth of a sixteen-year-old girl. Yet there are barriers as with any goals in life. Plans needed to be made, including adding multiple scenarios and options. Together, we broke everything down. She was clear on her career path, athletic desires, and location requirements yet didn't fully understand the financial hardships of some of her desired choices. When we explored the financial responsibility, scholarship possibilities, opportunities for skiing, proximity to her family, and career choice, her realistic options became clear. We made a plan. She knows exactly what her ski schedule looks like, how much money she needs to save, which scholarships she needs to apply for, and how to overcome obstacles that could possibly derail her from her path. Simple as that.

If only it were that easy when we wanted something ourselves. When we're faced with what stands between us and what we want, we get uncomfortable.

The Surprising Truth about Expectations

Am I being self-centered? Do I really know what I'm doing? Do I even deserve this? Is it worth it?

I say *enough*. If a sixteen-year-old can create a plan and execute, so can we. It's time we align our expectations and our abilities so we can finally get what we want out of life. After all, most of the time, the excuse "but I don't know how to do that" is *so* untrue. You already have experience doing these things for other people. It's not that different to do them for yourself. We ladies are professional expectation fulfillers. Everyone in our lives expects things from us. Nowadays you can't just be a mom. You have to be a mom *and* a career woman. You cook dinner, go to yoga, run your kids to basketball games, carpool, and do your family's laundry, all in a two-hour period. We juggle so many balls in the air, one false step could send them all tumbling down. Yet many women have low expectations around self-care and their sweet spot. Let's look at the expectations others have of us as a challenge. Raise your standards when it comes to putting yourself first. I know you already have the skills to do that. You're already putting everyone else first (because they expect you to), and you do a dang good job of it.

Expectations—I don't blame you if you feel like that little word has negative connotations. It sucks that women carry way more than our fair share of them. That said, I believe you can either let those expectations wear you down or fire you up. I made a conscious choice to stop letting them wear me down. I'd love to tell you I did it all by myself. I didn't. So who taught me what it means to shift expectations into opportunities? It might surprise you.

PUT DOWN YOUR DANG PHONE AND WATCH YOUR KIDS: A LESSON ON EXPECTATIONS

You've probably heard the old saying, "Mom knows best." You've probably found yourself saying, "Because I said so, and I'm the mom." Let me tell you something I've learned as a mother of two and stepmother of four. To survive in today's expectations-driven world, we have to stop and watch our kids. They're the most resilient people you'll ever meet. I watch how my kids fight to meet expectations. I'm in awe of their willingness to get back up after a fall. It's like they know what has to be done— so they do it.

We spend every free minute reading articles shared on social media about how to be better, happier women. Instead, let's put down our phones and watch what our kids are doing.

When you're a parent, the advice you give your kids isn't only for them. You should listen, too. I wish I'd taken

The Surprising Truth about Expectations

my own advice sooner. When my stepdaughter asked for help to plan the next several years of her life, she made me realize that planning applies to everything in life. By creating a plan with the steps you need to follow, you set expectations for yourself. And living up to the expectations you carry for yourself is the fastest path to happiness, fulfillment, and most of all, to your sweet spot. And if your family knows you can be successful, they're going to hold you to those expectations. Not because you're not enough but because they want you to achieve your dreams as much as you do.

Thankfully, I now see expectations as a form of empowerment. What my family, friends, and business partners expect me to do for them is like a mirror. Instead of feeling bogged down by them, I let them show me everything I'm capable of. I step up when my people need me. For example, I love that my son expects me to pick him up from school every day instead of taking the bus so we can talk on the drive home. It's not that he's not capable of riding the bus or walking. It's the time spent together that he needs.

All these expectations show me that I can live bigger and better in whatever role I have. I'm fortunate because owning my own business allows me to choose my own adventure. I love that when I wake up in the morning I ask myself, *What will my role be today? What adventures will today bring, and how can I best enjoy them?* Some days I get to be an awesome mom, and that's my only job. Some days I get to be this amazing business owner who helps my partners achieve more than what they even thought was possible. There is no reason why I have to choose mom over business owner or vice versa—I wanted it all, and I *expected* myself to make it happen. Just writing about it makes me happy. I'm doing what I want to be doing. I *want* to be working. I *want* to be cooking dinner for my kiddos. I *want* to go out and brush my horses. I *want* to exceed every expectation people in my life have of me and set high hopes for my self-care, too.

    Embracing and celebrating those expectations also means being realistic about what you can and cannot do. Let's be real, raw, and humble with ourselves. At this point in my life, I can pretty much tell you that if I have a goal, it's as good as done. I'm driven, I'm a planner, and I keep things real. Many don't share my aspirations, and that's OK. All that matters is what matters to you and what you're willing (or not willing) to give up to get it.

    For example, if you want to get more involved in your kids' lives, are you willing to open your home to their friends and host age-appropriate parties? Invite them to join you for activities you know they'll enjoy? Support their creative self-expression even if it looks different from what you would do? It's up to you to choose what matters most to you. Decide what you're willing to give up to make it happen. Maybe that means taking a night off from yoga to cook dinner as a family. Is it worth it?

What you want and what you're willing to give up to get it will change as you get older. There are things I was willing to give up in my twenties that I'm not willing to give up now. When I was young, I was adventurous and a bit indecisive. I wanted a little of this and a little of that. I was "just OK" at everything, but I wasn't great at anything. I couldn't get myself focused. My goals are much clearer now. I know I want to be an amazing business owner by day and, come 4:00 p.m. when my kids walk through the door, an amazing mom.

It's easy to look at someone else's situation and see the path you'd take. It's not so easy when you're making choices for yourself. Think about everything you've done for other people in the past week. Your boss, your coworkers, your spouse, your kids, your girlfriends, your kids' school. Close your eyes and remember every little thing you did for someone other than yourself.

Now imagine what it would look like to do some of those things *just for you*. Take the expectations others have of you and flip them into expectations for your own self-care. Did you finish a project, make time this weekend, or make coffee for your partner? If so, then sit down and enjoy some coffee yourself.

Did you take your kid out for ice cream? If so, then get a pedicure or massage for all the awesome things you've accomplished. Expectations don't have to be big and scary anymore.

CHAPTER 7
WHO'S ON YOUR TEAM?

You know what I hate most about the little witch? When she's whispering her lies, excuses, and objections in your ear, you often hear people you trust repeat her. It could be your best girlfriend, a parent, even your partner or spouse. As women, we're always seeking approval. We want to know that our circle of influence has our back. That's not always the case.

Let's talk real for a second. I want you to think of that one friend. The one you secretly crave approval from yet can't seem to get a second glance from no matter what you do. She's not there to pat you on the back or offer a genuine high five. When you're good, she's nowhere to be found. But when life sucks, she invites you over for Friday night cocktails. Misery loves company, the saying goes. No matter how terrible the relationship is, we still chase that friend's approval. We want her to congratulate us on leaving our marriage, growing our business, raising amazing kids, and sticking up for ourselves. I know what you're thinking. *Is she really writing this? Is she really saying that grown women seek the same acceptance from friends and family our teenage daughters do?* Yes, friend, it's real. It never goes away.

Is that your story? Sometimes it's hard to surround yourself with people who truly understand how to support you, whether that means congratulating you for earning that big promotion or taking the kids out so you can slide into the bathtub. You can't be successful and *not* feel good, yet some people in your life want you to feel *bad*. You need people who celebrate you. It's time to say goodbye to people who keep bringing you down. Making your sweet spot your new norm means raising your standards.

Now, don't start looking for a divorce lawyer or tell your mother you never want to speak to her again. The unsupportive people closest to us aren't that way on purpose. There is a way to love the most important people in your life while attracting the support you need to get to your sweet spot—and stay there forever.

THE DAY I REALIZED I WAS SNOOTY (AND RAISED MY PERSONAL STANDARDS)

On a kid-free date, my husband and I drove around for an hour trying to find a restaurant we could agree on. Every place we passed, I had a reason not to eat there. After the fourth restaurant, Mike joked, "You're so snooty. Since when did you become so snooty?"

I'd never thought of myself as *that* person. Then I remembered one of the first things my doctor said to me after my cancer diagnosis.

"Anyone or anything toxic in your life has to find a new home. No more stress."

This got me thinking. What in my life wasn't serving me well? Who wasn't showing up and supporting me on my journey? What was causing more stress than joy in my life? It became clear. Some things had to change. Just to be clear, it's not that these relationships or my situation were necessarily bad. Take my career, for instance. I loved teaching. It just wasn't serving me for what I desired in my life for my family. Similar to some relationships. These also weren't bad. They just weren't serving me in the ways I needed in order to thrive.

I remembered all of this as we finally agreed on a restaurant and circled the parking lot for a spot.

"It's not that I'm snooty," I told Mike. "It's that I've raised my standards. That goes for the people who get to be in my life, the food I eat, the places I go, the things I do, the trips I take . . . " I sighed. "Time is precious. I have high standards for what I do with it."

I hope you take that to heart, my friend. I want you to raise your standards, too. As should everyone who sees themselves living a better life than they currently are. What we surround ourselves with has to align with what we see ourselves doing. Otherwise we won't feel supported, and we surely won't get what we want in life. If you aspire too high, the downward peer pressure of toxic people will keep your standards low and your achievements lower.

I want to roll with people who make me aspire to more. In my circle of influence, I take a lot of pride in the people I hang out with. I don't pal around with toxic people. I'm not going to associate with somebody who is needy or who brings me down. I look for people who lift me up and force me out of my comfort zone so I can be a bigger and better person.

I always tell my girlfriends, "My circle of influence has to be cooler than I am." They think that's funny. I think it's the truth. If I'm going to spend an hour at lunch with someone, I want to leave thinking, *That was the best hour I've spent all day.* As busy women, it's crucial we value our time. Part of respecting that is choosing who we spend time with. I'm not going to get on a phone call with someone who makes me feel like jumping off a cliff. Otherwise I'd rather be playing with my kids.

Does this make me snooty? Maybe. Does this mentality pay off? You bet it does. It's about alignment. I want to grow with people who are interested in the same thing. We "get" each other. We know how to help each other because we're walking in each other's shoes every single day. That's what every woman wants—to go the same direction with like-minded people. It's only in these relationships that we'll find the support, encouragement, and love we need and deserve.

LEVEL UP YOUR CIRCLE OF INFLUENCE

You can't choose your family other than spouse and kiddos. (Well, kinda. You get what I mean.) But we can all choose our friends. Your circle of influence doesn't fall into your lap. Curate these relationships well. How? How do you find people who make you feel good about yourself? Search for them. Look outside your routine. Have kids? Hang out with their moms. Love the outdoors? Connect with your local hiking Meetup group. Want to learn a new skill alongside others? Find classes near you. Thinking about starting a part-time business? Join or start a mastermind for other aspiring entrepreneurs to share tips.

Filling your circle with people who build you up rather than tear you down is a little like dating. (If you're thinking, *But it's been twenty years since I dated*, hang with me for a second. You'll get it.) Meeting new people is hard at first—you win some and you lose some—but when you put yourself out there, your confidence skyrockets. The energy you give to others is the energy you get back in return.

Does that mean you should dump friends and family who take more than they give? Not at all. You know better than anyone if there is someone (or a few someones) who brings you down. If you see their face and nod your head right now, then it's probably time to part ways for a season. *A season.* Loved ones who aren't aligned with your new direction in life don't need "space" or the silent treatment. Your spouse may not understand your needs and your goals because you haven't made them clear. Your mom can't read your mind. Before you move across town to avoid your needy sister, try giving her a great self-help book (like this one) with a bow around it. Tell her, "Get your poop in a group and call me in two weeks after you read this. I love you, and I'm on a mission to live a better life. This is how you can best support me on that mission." Honor what feels good to you while loving the people in your life. Not everyone will jump on the sweet spot train, and that's OK—as long as they don't stop you from boarding.

Who's on Your Team?

Always love people where they're at. I learned that from the women I met on my first naked spa adventure.

My what?!

Haven't you heard?

Naked spa day.

It's a thing.

EVERY WOMAN NEEDS NAKED SPA DAY

It was my six-year cancer-free anniversary. I was in Atlanta for a business conference and just so happened to be staying next door to a favorite restaurant I frequented in Bozeman often. Ted's Montana Grill. I was sitting with a girlfriend chatting about life when the waitress placed a coaster in front of me and asked what I'd like to drink. The card featured a one-line quote from John Wayne.

Courage is being scared to death but saddling up anyway.[4]

---

[4] John W. Whitehead, "John Wayne Was True Grit," HuffPost, August 6, 2011, www.huffpost.com/entry/john-wayne-was-true-grit_b_871965.

Life has no coincidences. This wasn't the first time this quote appeared in my life. Six years prior, this same coaster appeared before me. I casually scooped it up and put it in the visor of my car. A friendly reminder of everything I was about to embark on as I fought cancer.

The conference brought me insights into life, business, friendships, best practices, and the sad news that my friend's father passed away.

"I need to clear some space in my head," she said. "I know we're supposed to be getting ready for that luau party for all the participants, but I'm going to take some time for myself. You go on without me."

"No. No way," I said. "I'm not leaving you alone at the hotel. The luau can go on without us. Let's go to a spa. I'll meet you in our room in ten minutes."

She nodded. We all knew what she needed right then. I rallied the other girls we were staying with and asked them to find the perfect place to relax our friend. We ended up at a Korean spa, which I knew nothing about. We walked in and paid for four steam room massages. The receptionist handed us each a bulky orange outfit that looked like a prison jumpsuit. What was happening?

Who's on Your Team?

"You put this on, and then you go in." She pointed to a set of opaque glass doors that stretched floor to ceiling.

We changed in the ladies' locker room and walked into the steam room. There were probably thirty women of all colors, sizes, shapes, and nationalities walking around. Every single one was completely naked.

A wave of panic made me gasp. I don't walk around naked with other women on a regular basis. Or ever. I was afraid of what these women would think when they saw my scars. *Are they going to stare at me? Will they feel sorry for me? Are they going to ask me questions about what happened? What will they think of me?*

After my double mastectomy, I felt like my femininity had been stripped away. Now here I was walking into a spa to expose myself to the world. Excuses to get the hell out of there ran through my mind. *A headache. The flu. Excuse myself to the restroom and climb out the window. No. Don't be a coward.* I shook my head. My friend needed me. I wasn't going to bail on her now.

I took a deep breath and unwrapped my jumpsuit. *Find your power. Find your strength. You can do this. No one's going to judge you. That was cancer; this wasn't a choice. It's not your fault you look this way.* And there I was, butt naked in the steam room along with all these other women. *Holy. Crap. I did it. There's no turning back now.* That's when I realized all these other women were doing the same thing I was. They were battered. They were scarred. They weren't perfect. Yet they showed up. They showed up in strength. In love. In power. I felt so at peace. It was the most magical, amazing, loving situation I've ever been in. There was absolutely no separation. We had our massage right in the middle of the room. And our body scrub. Nobody was there to judge. No one questioned who we were or what we were doing. No one knew anything about each other. That's when it hit me.

This is the circle of influence I want in my life.

I wish every woman could experience what I did that day. I left the spa with a better understanding of the beautiful female experience. When we stop worrying about being perfect, that's when the magic happens. Everyone is equal, and no one is judged. The next day at the convention, several of the speakers delivered the same clear message: *stop comparing yourself to others.* Coincidence? I don't think so.

CHAPTER 8
SWEETEN THE SPOT

The sweet spot. You know what it is, how to get there, and why you deserve it. You have the courage to seize self-care moments throughout the day every day. You protect your precious resources such as time and energy. You have the skills you need to get what you truly want out of life. And you're surrounding yourself with judgment-free women who support your journey. Congratulations!

Or should I say welcome?

As in . . .

Welcome to your sweet spot.

The Sweet Spot

This is what it's all about. You're here because you've cleared the baggage and conquered the excuses that keep you from enjoying those little things that just make you happy. You've evicted the little witch, celebrated everything you've achieved, and disrupted your status quo. You're time blocking, setting clear expectations for yourself, and curating your circle of influence. And now, your sweet spot is becoming your new norm—whatever that looks like for you. That child-free spouse date. Bath time with wine. A side business you can call your own. It doesn't matter how small the gift you give yourself or how big self-help experts tell you to dream. That's the beauty of your sweet spot. It is whatever you want it to be.

Now that you've got those little things that just make you happy, what do you want next? Finding your sweet spot is a little like raising kids. With your first child, you don't quite get it. When your second child comes along, you know what to do without asking Mom or a search engine. You're not constantly panicking. Self-care is no different. You feel guilty for wanting a little extra money to buy a cute pair of jeans. But you earned them. So you buy the jeans and feel good about your purchase. Now you're ready for more . . . guilt-free. A goal achieved opens up a new goal. A sweet spot enjoyed makes more space for new accomplishments, new experiences, and new pleasures. So, what's it going to be? What are the things that make you happy?

Sweeten the Spot

That's right, sister. You started out dreaming small, but you've mastered that. Now I'm asking you to unleash your imagination. Because you're ready for those big dreams now. What dream comes next? Maybe you've worked self-care moments into your day, but you want to afford experiences like weekly massages. What does it look like to increase your income? It could be starting a side business, positioning yourself for a promotion, or making a plan to shift to a higher-paying industry. Whatever the case, it's time to upgrade. To sweeten your sweet spot. And keep sweetening it. Here's what will happen.

Think of that woman you know who just radiates happiness. You crave her round-the-clock sense of accomplishment. She's always calm in a crisis and fierce in a competition. You know what these women have in common?

They keep.

Dreaming.

Bigger.

They don't live loud, then get quiet. They don't splurge on self-care for a season, then sacrifice free time for their spouse and kids' demands. And most of all, they don't settle into comfort when they know they can transition to bigger and better. That can be your story, too. You can go wherever your dreams take you.

When I was a girl, I wanted to travel in a convertible with my soul mate. That's my reality now. All because I dreamed bigger than my current situation. When I got diagnosed with cancer, the *only* thing that could make me happy was showing my kids what a healthy, loving relationship looked like. *I'm not dying until my kids see what love really is.* Amazingly, I found my soul mate at the Phoenix airport, and he changed my world.

When I started my business, I knew I needed to make five grand a month to quit my job, leave my husband, and get top-notch cancer care. I needed to know my bills would be paid in whatever situation my family and I found ourselves. I mapped it out, so I knew exactly what I needed to do. If I could make that happen, I could change my life. I did that and a lot more. On top of that, I've partnered with many amazing women who do the same.

When you commit to sweetening your sweet spot, life gets a lot more fun. It's exciting to transition from little things that just make you happy to the big stuff. Of course, big is relative. Some people want to feel good when they look in the mirror. So they follow this book, kick down the blocks, and find a delicious meal plan they can follow. Maybe your sweet spot upgrade is going on a kids-free spa date with your girlfriends once a month. You achieve that and feel the sweet spot. Again, the sweet spot looks different for everyone. For me, it's curling up in a warm blanket on my deck and watching the sunset tuck into the mountain after a long, amazing day. It's going to work every day knowing that I'm helping other women make a difference. And it's building an amazing future for our family alongside my soul mate. This is what the sweet spot looks like for me now, but it's not where I started.

THE FIVE UPGRADES

The number one mistake I see people make while doing the little things that just make them happy is treating them like permanent markers. Take that pressure off yourself. Every time you hit a goal (yay!), take time to rework and reassess. And here's the scoop on how that works. Each time you sit down to design the next part of your self-care-filled life, be sure to dig into the five categories that affect who you are and who you want to be.

YOURSELF

If I've said it once, I've said it a hundred times: everything starts with self-care. It's not selfish or inconsiderate—it's the exact opposite.

The number one way to design a self-care-filled life is to intentionally think about how you're going to take care of yourself. Maybe it looks like nightly bubble baths or maybe it means signing up for that yoga class downtown. Either way, making yourself a priority in your life will set the foundation for everything else.

MARRIAGE

If you're married, you know that if this relationship isn't solid, nothing else is. When you're designing your self-care-filled life, be sure to think about how your spouse fits into it.

Do you want more date nights? Do you wish you could travel with them on their business trips? Would you love to set time aside for that couples cruise you keep seeing advertised? Yes, your marriage is a form of self-care.

RELATIONSHIPS

Although your relationships with yourself and your spouse are critical, so are the relationships with other people in your life. This can include your family, kiddos, and circle of influence.

Is there a friend you've been dying to have coffee with? Call them up. Would you love to start a monthly "family" dinner tradition with your closest friends? Set it up. Set aside ten minutes a day to check in with a friend over a text or social media direct message. The people around you are a huge part of your life, so don't forget to include them when designing your self-care-filled life.

EATING WELL AND EXERCISING

I don't know about you, but if I don't plan my workouts and my healthy meals, they don't happen. If I want to go to an afternoon yoga class or trail ride, I have to actively block the time out to do it. And if I want to try that new grilled chicken recipe, I have to head to the store and buy the ingredients.

Eating well and exercising are the foundations to feeling amazing—which is critical to maximize self-care in your life. So when you're deciding how you want your life to look, be sure to think these out. Plus, when you do the work ahead of time, it doesn't seem like such a big deal to center your week around those two spin classes or afternoon walks with a friend.

MONEY

Yikes. I know, it's not always a fun topic to talk about. But being intentional with money is oh-so-critical when it comes to designing a self-care-filled life. For instance, if you know you want to travel more with your spouse or sign up for a meal-to-door delivery, your budget will have to adjust.

Putting yourself in control of your budget from the beginning will ease your stress and pull you out of a bad cycle. It'll also give you some time to decide what's important and structure everything else around that.

The Sweet Spot

If you're new to budgeting (and maybe just the word makes your hair stand on end), I'll let you in on a little secret. You can pull out your phone right now and create a Google Sheet with your goals, monthly income, and expenses written out. It's super simple and keeps you in check.

If you can get these five categories aligned, everything else will fall into place. Just remember—your sweet spot isn't a final destination. It's the act of leading an intentional life and getting clear on what's fulfilling for you. If you're truly happy, you won't be bored—even if you're not in your dream job yet. Continually checking in on those five categories will allow you to fully show up no matter where you are in your journey to your sweet spot.

At the end of the day, success isn't perfection. I don't expect you to put into practice everything you've read in this book all at once. Just look at me. I was a little choppy for the first forty-four years of life. We all are and all should be. The great transition from little things to big dreams is good, but it's not all roses. Learning a new skill like gardening is hard. Nobody said building a business was easy. Maybe meal planning is harder than you thought. That's why you want to keep those little things in your life. They're mini self-care moments throughout your day that boost your energy so you can go after the big stuff.

Meeting the love of my life was amazing. So was overcoming cancer. And building a successful business from home. Yet where I find true happiness is taking ten minutes to garden, locking my door for a bath, and feeling proud (not guilty) of everything I've achieved. The sweetest spot of all is a mix of the little things that just make you happy and the big dreams that make your heart pound out of your chest. I give you permission to have it all.

A NONNEGOTIABLE CONTRACT

I know what you're thinking.

How, Kacie? How do I claim "it all"? Where do I go from here?

Whether you want the kids-free nap or the Tuesday golf day, I want you to make a nonnegotiable sweet spot contract with yourself. For the next ninety days, you're going to commit to _____ (fill in the blank!). Whatever your self-care experience looks like, it's nonnegotiable. A no-matter-what-I'm-doing-it kind of thing. Don't be vague. *I'm going to be nice to the kids* or *I'm going to take time for myself* aren't tangible. Make your commitment specific, like, *I'm going to go grocery shopping and prep meals for the week every Sunday* or *I'm going to join that new yoga studio and go to class twice a week*. Commit for ninety days, and you will see results. Your intentions turned into decisions. Your hopes turned into habits. Your dreams turned into your reality. All in ninety days. That's the beauty of commitment.

I've found that telling your circle of influence what you're up to helps it stick. Tell your girlfriends about your ninety-day commitment to find your sweet spot. Let them know they deserve to be happy, too. As women, we don't hear the truth often enough. Like you, me, and every other woman on the face of the earth, the ladies in your life hear the little witch's lies, too. Go tell them the truth. It's your duty. Besides, what's the worst that could happen? Nothing less than greatness. As women, when we find something life changing, we share it. When we find a good opportunity, we share it. When we find a product that works, we share it.

If we can leave a positive impact on just one person, why wouldn't we? Share your sweet spot with your world and more of your world will find their sweet spots, too. Most things in life are better when shared with other people. I love nothing more than when my kids watch me get up in the morning, work hard as an entrepreneur, and live my dreams. I know I'm nurturing a work ethic that will serve them for the rest of their lives. Whether you're sharing your sweet spot by example or telling everyone you know, expect *greatness* to happen.

THE CALL TO GREATNESS

A few months ago, I attended a women's leadership convention. I always expect to learn one amazing thing at these events. Don't get me wrong—the entire event was amazing. But at this point in my career, it takes a lot to get my butterflies fluttering and my heart thumping. On the fourth day, my moment came.

A panel of speakers shared from the heart how it felt to truly serve and be an influencer in the world. On the panel was this powerhouse woman who spoke for thirty minutes with certainty, love, and kindness. Her closing statement was the gem I needed.

"Be great now."

Wow. *Be great now*. Not tomorrow. Not next year. *Now*.

I've read a gazillion articles about how overworked, overstretched, overcommitted, and just plain *over* things we are. When we're not in the sweet spot, we live our lives with half-assed accomplishments and excuses for why we can't figure this world out.

So be great *now*. "OK" or even "pretty good" don't feed the soul. And it sure won't help you expand your sweet spot for bigger dreams and better things. You and I weren't placed on this earth to play small. We need passion. Excitement. Butterflies.

Comfort? It's time to kick it to the curb.

On a recent trip to Switzerland, I was reminded once again what being great and living life to its fullest is all about. When we arrived in Interlaken, our tour guide asked us to choose daily adventures. They ranged from a train ride across the Alps to shopping excursions to paragliding. I checked the box next to the train ride. *Safe.*

"So, what did you pick?" my friend Emily asked me.

"Train."

She shot me a glare.

"What?" I asked her.

"Kacie, do you want to go home and tell your kids you rode a train, or do you want to experience this beautiful country in a way you'll never forget?" She held up her own form and pointed to the box she'd checked.

"Paragliding? Uh, I'm terrified of heights, and I'm, uh . . ." I stammered. "The train sounded fun, I can take pictures—"

"Forget pictures. Live a little. What do you say? I'm not taking no for an answer."

That was the day I ditched playing small and maybe safe as well. I jumped off that mountain, and I never looked back. I may have even puked a little, but hey, I jumped. And I'm glad I did.

Be great now.

Commit with me today. Take a big, deep breath. You're armed and ready. You have everything you need to make your sweet spot even sweeter. Now it's time to go live.

You got this, sister.

ABOUT THE AUTHOR

Kacie Vaudrey is an author, coach, and entrepreneur serving over 110,000 women on their journey to find their purpose, passion, and sweet spot. As a successful network marketer, Kacie helps women create an intentional lifestyle around their goals and desires. *The Sweet Spot: Everything Women Need to Know to Enjoy Life More* gives women permission to enjoy life more. Kacie's first book, *The Essentials: Everything Women Need to Know to Make It as a Network Marketer*, and its companion, *The Essential Planner: The Only Self-Care Planner and Network Marketing Workbook for Women Who Want It All*, show women how to build a profitable network marketing business inside their sweet spot without sacrificing why they're doing it in the first place . . . even while running around with the kids. Whether you want a radical career change or just a little extra money for your family trip to Disney, Kacie can help you follow your passion. Create your intentional lifestyle at www.KacieVaudrey.com.

www.ingramcontent.com/pod-product-compliance
Lightning Source LLC
LaVergne TN
LVHW041229080426
835508LV00011B/1121